WHY TRADERS
FAIL

Planning Your Way to Success

Joseph J. Mertes

DISCLOSURES

LEGAL INFORMATION

Any information, data, statements, opinions, or projections made in any materials, newsletter, website ("Website"), seminar, mentoring or training program, or any other communication, service, or product, whether written or verbal (collectively, the "Materials"), affiliated with Joseph James LLC ("Joseph James"), may contain certain forward looking statements, projections and information that are based on the beliefs of Joseph James as well as assumptions made by, and information currently available to, Joseph James. Such statements in the Materials reflect the view of Joseph James with respect to future events and are subject to certain risks, uncertainties and assumptions. Should one or more of these risks or uncertainties materialize, or should underlying assumptions prove incorrect, actual results may vary materially from those described in the Materials. Furthermore, although carefully verified, data is not guaranteed as to accuracy or completeness. Any quotations of individuals other than the authors or providers of the Materials are provided for informational purposes only and their accuracy and veracity are not guaranteed. The statements, opinions, and/or data expressed in the Materials are subject to change without notice based on market and other conditions. The Materials are based on information available as of the time they were written, provided, or communicated and Joseph James disclaims any duty to update the Materials and any content, research or information contained therein. Accordingly, neither Joseph James nor its principals or affiliates make any representation as to the timeliness of any information in the Materials. As a result of all of the foregoing, inter alia, neither Joseph James nor its principals can be held responsible for trades executed by the recipients or viewers of the Materials based on the statements, projections, research, or any other information of any other kind included therein. Investments in securities are speculative and involve a high degree of risk; you should be aware that you could lose all or a substantial amount of your investment if you attempt to apply any of the information in the Materials.

COPYRIGHT

Cover and Book Design by: Kathleen Scott | Breadcrumbs Studio
www.breadcrumbsstudio.com

TABLE OF CONTENTS

INTRODUCTION

Having graduated from college, I wanted to work for a year or two before heading to law school. My first real job was with an attorney who did tax and investment planning for wealthy clients. As part of his services, he actually formed the entities his clients invested in. Looking back, it was really a small private venture capital firm. My position was to operate the acquired entities for a profit. My plan was to work for two years and then I was off to law school.

What I learned was a tremendous amount about tax strategies, investment planning and more importantly, capital formation. With two years complete, I started taking law classes during the summer to get a head start. I was surprised to discover the legal profession was not for me. At the end of the summer I realized I didn't want to be the guy who documented other peoples deals. I wanted to be the guy who made the deals. Immediately, I transferred to the business school and started a two year program to get an MBA.

Degree in hand, I ventured into my own business of analyzing investment opportunities and raising capital for their acquisition. Along the way, my attention was always drawn toward the financial markets. After twenty years in venture capital, I closed the office and became a full time trader and investor, although I continue to dabble in capital formation. In each venture I formed, there was extensive analysis and planning. More importantly, there was always an exit strategy.

The venture capital business can be very draining. Having played soccer in college, I decided to take some time off and ended up getting involved in competitive youth soccer. During this time, I was basically supporting myself through trading in the financial markets.

One evening I was coaching a very competitive team and was headed for my car. Earlier that day, I made a substantial amount of money trading NASDAQ futures. As I walked past one of the cars, I noticed a parent. He was a doctor and his child was on the team I had just coached. He caught my attention because he was holding a newsletter that had technical charts. I tried to get a closer glimpse of what he was reading. My curiosity finally got the best of me.

I asked if he was a trader as well as a doctor. He explained that he managed his own portfolio and retirement plan. He was in the process of educating himself to manage his own money as a second business and hoped one day to leave the medical profession and just trade his own account. I let the conversation stop there. I figured it was best that he only see me as a soccer coach. But, the seeds of an idea had sprouted.

I spent a career in venture capital, analyzing various deals, raising capital, doing workouts of troubled companies and restructuring capital. In each case the development of a sound business plan was critical. I reflected on my own trading, which I had been doing for over twenty years. Not once had I considered preparing a business plan, even though I had prepared many over the years for other ventures. The doctor's statement on trading as a business stuck a chord.

Questions began to form. Where was I going with my own trading? What were my goals and objectives? Was I organized for real success? Did I have good control procedures? If some larger firm wanted to acquire what I was doing, was the business setup properly? What if I wanted to acquire capital and really grow the business? Was I doing the things that would allow me to choose that option?

A business plan defines success. It is a road map of where you want to go and the steps you need to take to get there. I had not defined any of that. I simply wanted to make money, as most traders and investors do. More importantly, was I planning for the unexpected? A business plan is a control function. If you are not meeting the objectives in the plan, then corrective action needs to be taken. It is a warning system.

As the questions flooded my thoughts, answers were flowing just as fast. My excitement grew. Returning to my home office, I started to make an outline of the steps I had taken in the past to analyze prospective ventures. However, this time, I was doing a startup of a trading business: My Trading Business. Once the process began, I couldn't stop. At 4:00 in the morning, I had pages of outlines and thoughts. After a little sleep, I knew I had the making of a sound business plan. It would take many more hours of thought and writing but that plan would eventually lead me to more success in trading and teaching others how to start and develop a successful business of trading and investing.

In many instances I will use the term trader and investor. Unfortunately, there are some who misconstrue the term trader to mean only a day trader. While that may tend to intimidate some, if you are an intermediate or longer term investor, you are still a trader, since you trade in the various instruments you choose. If you are a day trader, you are an investor. You invest in specific instruments but your choice is to hold them for a very short time period.

Ben Franklin once said, "If you fail to plan, you plan to fail". As you read this book, I hope you will find it thought provoking. After all, how many businesses would you invest in where you sit down at a computer, click a mouse and try to compete in one of the most competitive environments there is without some sort of plan? It is important to recognize, each time you enter a market, there is someone on the other side of that trade who thinks you are wrong and is trying to take your money. More importantly, the only way you can make money is to take it from someone else.

There are various ways to prepare a business plan. Some will choose a formal plan and follow the concepts of this book strictly. Others will choose a less formal approach and jot down a few pages of notes. Whatever works for you, do it. It is critical to remember that once your plan is complete, it doesn't go into a file for future reference. It is the instrument in which you will define success or failure and will give you the early warning signals, if a re-evaluation needs to occur and corrective action taken.

Your plan is a living organism. It changes and develops with the business environment, the economic environment and governmental agencies. More importantly, the plan changes as you operate the business. You will find all through the book references to the shareholders and the employees. In any business it is the shareholders who must keep the employees accountable for success. As an individual trader or investor, we must do both. We must be the employee of our business and do the things to make it successful. But, we also must be the shareholder and hold the employee accountable for planned performance. As the shareholder, you must give the employee the knowledge, training and tools necessary to produce success. And you will find, periodically the shareholder will have to take the employee out to the woodshed for stern talking to.

Albert Einstein said the definition of insanity was doing the same thing over and over and expecting a different result. I have worked with many individuals who keep doing the same thing over and over and lacking the success they thought was easily achieved.

- "Tomorrow will be a better day."
- "Forget today, I just didn't feel right."
- "I should have noticed that pattern before making the entry. Tomorrow will be better."
- "I should have exited that trade sooner."
- "The market has to come back in my direction tomorrow. I am in so deep now, I can't get out."

These and many more are all excuses I have heard. Once I was called by a client from Europe. He explained he was in a trade and the market had gone against him. Instead of exiting the trade at his planned stop, he "felt" the market would recover, so he held his position. The market kept falling. Then it fell some more. When he finally called me, he had lost thousands and was panicking. He asked for help.

By the end of that day, we had recovered almost all of his losses. Before hanging up with him, I told him to schedule a flight to come to the US. He asked why and I explained that he needed to come and spend time refreshing what I had taught him in the past. He complained the flight would be too expensive. I reminded him what he almost lost that day. He scheduled the trip and we spent a good time going back over the control procedures that are critical for success. He went on to be a successful trader. What he forgot was the differentiation between employee and shareholder. The shareholder did not hold the employee accountable. The result almost cost the shareholder a lot of money.

If you are an individual managing you own money or someone who wants to build a trading business, it is critical you prepare a sound business plan as the shareholder of the business. When you are ready to execute on that plan, it is critical the employee follow the plan. All plans change and you will find yours may need revising and changing monthly. That is perfect.

There are two distinct aspects of entering this business whether you are full time or part time. The first is the preparation of a well thought out business plan. The second is the development of a sound strategy and tactic that you will use in approaching the markets. This is the trade plan. I will touch briefly on a sound strategy but that will be dealt with in more detail in another book. After years of trading, making my own mistakes and in working with clients, I have found most of us do not know when or how to change our behavior. After all, there is no one to hold us accountable except ourselves. There is no mechanism for accountability. Therefore, most keep doing the same things over and over and getting the same lackluster results.

The industry suggests that 92% of traders fail. That means only 8% make money. I suggest those who succeed have done some form of planning and control. They hold themselves accountable and make important changes to their behavior when necessary. Your plan will give you control of your business and let you know when you will need to take corrective action. It will make you disciplined.

As you begin reading, open your mind to the fact you are entering a new business. Feel free to design this business the way you want, but remember, you must have a vehicle for determining success or failure. Your plan is that vehicle. Only you can decide on what is success and what is failure.

If your approach is like mine used to be and you come into each day just wanting to make money, then look at your capital account. Are you making what you really expect? When you take a loss, do you simply brush it off and come back the next day without taking any action? If you do, then you are increasing the probabilities dramatically that you will be in the 92% of people who fail.

Alternatively, if you have a plan and hold to it, you will increase the probabilities of being in the 8% of successful investors. If you go to work for a bank or a fund, do you think they will just tell you to make money? Of course not. They will give you specific goals and objectives. Why should you treat your own capital and business differently? More importantly, if you do not achieve those goals and objectives, they will not simply ignore you and tell you tomorrow will be a better day. They take you aside and work with you to improve performance. They will want to see corrective action taken. Why not treat your own capital and business the same way?

CHAPTER 1

THE PURPOSE OF PLANNING

T HE MAIN PURPOSE OF planning for your investment business is summed up in one word: control. That word is extremely important. I believe the majority of traders fail due to a lack of control. Another way to define control is risk management.

The first questions I ask a client is, "why are you entering the investment business". Most give me a blank stare. I know, in their mind, they are thinking it's a strange question. The answers that eventually come are scattered, but most come down to wanting to be in control of their own money and they want to make more money than just investing for the long-term. I usually press the issue from there by asking them what they expect to gain from their efforts. Their body actions usually suggest they are becoming uncomfortable. It is obvious, they never really thought about the question of why. The thought of being in control of their own funds, making money with those funds, and becoming a stock market genius are all they see. So, ask yourself the question. What do you expect to achieve by entering the business of investing and trading? How do you see your life as a result of this business?

After considering the question deeply, begin to view your trading as a business start-up. Once you have done this and truly thought deeply about it, you will have taken the first step toward being a professional trader/investor.

It would be inconceivable for anyone to enter into a business without some type of planning. Some are more elaborate than others, but there is always a plan for those who strive for success. I venture to state: the greater success of new businesses goes to those who have a well thought out and written business plan. As a business owner, you need to know the market you are going into. You want to know the cost of your product. You want to define what your expected profitability will be. Finally, you will want a benchmark in which to evaluate yourself. In the business of trading and investing the control of the trade and control of the trader are the most important aspects of the planning process. That is not to diminish any of the other factors, but these are items that define success or failure.

Remember Ben Franklin said, "If you fail to plan, you plan to fail". Why is it that so many traders and investors enter markets with no plan at all? Could it be the same reason that most fail? I would say it is so. The ease of entry into this business and the allure of easy success cause most not to consider the most important aspect of starting a business and that is a plan for success. As a trader and investor, we have a tendency to be lazy and not do the work. It looks incredibly easy to see a trend that occurred and think all you have to do is buy the bottom and sell the top. If ninety-two percent of traders fail, then it must not be so easy. Remember, most of the work is done in the analysis stage. The entry and exit take only a split second. What happens after the entry is just as important as the decision process that leads up to it.

If you are serious about becoming a successful trader or investor, then you must accept the fact that it is going to take a lot of work. As I said previously, this is a highly competitive business. The only way you can make money is to take someone else's money. However, while you are thinking about taking theirs, they are spending hours doing the work necessary to take yours.

Recently, I was at the gym with my trainer. I was exhausted. Sweat was dripping from me. I was bent over gasping for air and looked up. Another guy had walked in to work out. He looked at me and smiled. I just shook my head. The trainer smiled, knowing he had driven me hard. The other guy asked me if I wanted to win. I paused for a moment, then he said again much louder, "Do you want to win? If you want to win, make it hurt some more. You're still standing, so give it more effort". I wanted to scream that I wasn't playing a game, but I immediately knew what he meant. If you want to compete then you have to work harder than your competitor. It is the same with trading and investing. If you want to be successful, you have to put in more work than the individual you are competing against.

If you simply sit down at a computer and expect to click a mouse and at the end of the day look at all of your profits, you are kidding yourself. There is another guy who spent most of the previous day studying, analyzing, researching and working harder than you. He/ she developed a trade plan and are following it. It is that person who is ready to take your money. When you spend a few hours doing the work, there is always someone else who stayed up most of the night to be better than you and take your money.

Just as any good program to workout begins with a plan for the month, the week and the day, so too it is with any business, especially the business of trading and investing. The planning begins with the business. First you have to develop a business plan. Next, you will develop a trade plan for each day. I will cover this in more detail later. From a business perspective, the trade plan is actually the operational plan.

Most basic management classes explain the four steps of the business process: planning, organization, management, control. Each step is critical to success. Important to you and any business are your control procedures. Control procedures bring us back to the planning process once again. Control procedures are even more important in the trade plan. Therefore, the first step is to draft a plan.

KEY REASONS TO PREPARE A PLAN

- A business plan provides a road map of where you are and where you want to go. Consider you are currently in a business profession and you want to start a second business of trading and investing your own money. Eventually, you want to get to the point where it will be your primary business. You might even have a vision of telling others of your prowess in the financial markets. If this is the case, then you know exactly what you will have to make to support yourself. You will have to establish a plan that will allow you to live off of your trading. If you are considering leaving your profession and making a living immediately, I highly recommend you reconsider, until you have completed the proper planning.

- Proper planning provides an opportunity for you to educate yourself. Much planning should go into how you will evaluate the markets and which markets (instruments) you will trade. You will need to plan your computer system, numbers of monitors, software packages to use, etc. You will need to consider what books you will read. You are going to be self-educating. Therefore, you will need to do some research on what you will study. I spent a lot of time studying Elliott Wave Theory. I can honestly say, I was an expert in counting waves, but then I found something that was even better. This was accomplished through continuing to study, read articles and books and talking to other professional traders. In other words you have to develop a methodology in which you will analyze the markets. That methodology will continue to morph, as the financial markets change.

- Years ago, when I was setting up my first professional system, I tried to think through all of the possible things that could happen while I was in a trade. This led me to buying battery backups that would give me plenty of time to save work or exit positions if the electricity went out. Probably the best part of my plan was redundant Internet connections. Back then I used a load balancing router. I had two different internet providers. The router balanced between whichever one was faster. One provider was always faster, but there were many times I would notice a slow down in the connection speed. I would look over at the modem and see the cable had gone out. The router automatically switched to the other provider. Except for the speed, I would have never known the cable was out. There were several times I was thankful for the planning I had done.

- Now I have a mobile hot spot on my cell phone. If there is an Internet disconnect, I turn on the hot spot and can connect my laptop, which is always charged, and can connect immediately. The battery backups are still in place.

- It will also be important to plan your methodology. In other words, how are you going to analyze the markets? Once you decide on a methodology, you will then be able to determine what software packages will suit you best. The software package you use will also determine the hardware you will need to run the package efficiently. Then you will test your methodology to see if it is valid.

- I use Time Price Opportunity (TPO) chart extensively in the strategy development. The best program I have found is Investor RT from Linnsoft (www.linsoft.com). I have found their charts to be the best and economical. The range of technical indicators is amazing and they are always developing new indicators.

- One final thought about methodology. There is no perfect system. All of the methodologies are good, but none perfect. There is no magic formula. If there is, it is called experience. While I don't use Elliot Wave Theory anymore, my knowledge and experience in it has helped me many times. Develop your own methodology. It is through trial and error that we gain experience. That experience will lead to increased profits. Remember to keep the cost of the error as low as possible: learn to manage risk.

- Planning provides an evaluation method that helps in determining courses of action. It defines success. If you are not achieving success, then it lets you know it is time for corrective action. I will cover this in more detail in the chapters on The Financial Plan and Controlling the Trader. But, I want to stress here, if you ignore everything else in this book, you should focus on developing a financial plan and control plan. Many traders and investors "crash and burn" because they did not know when to stop and re-evaluate their performance.

- It is important to understand that many things can and will get in your way of achieving success. I don't know why it is, but in the business of trading and investing, individuals seem to completely neglect the fact they are failing. I am sure there are some great psychological reasons for it, but there is only one thing that will trigger your shareholder self. That is looking at your financial plan and seeing the reality that you are not making your objectives. You will tell yourself tomorrow will be better. Trust me. It will not, unless you take corrective action. Corrective action is not taking a day off. Corrective action is taking the time necessary to study and find out why you are failing and then design corrective action.

- Simply blaming poor results on a bad day will not suffice. If it is a bad day, then take the day off. If your analysis is off, then figure out why it is off. There must be a trigger that makes you step back from the battle and assess what is going on. The methodology I use for analyzing markets is what I call Market Development and Market Structure. I basically analyze markets in multiple time frames and establish support and resistance areas in those time frames. I can then determine the strength or weakness of a trend going into those Key Reference Areas (KRA), as I call them. More on this later.

- There was a time not long ago that I had to adapt the way I analyzed the markets using the above methodology. For the most part the Stock Indices, which I was trading, kept moving into upper KRAs on weak internals. Instead of reversing, they would push through them without strengthening. I found I was not making trades because the expected rotations down were not occurring. Because I was not trading, I was not making the returns I had set as my objective. I had to stop and figure out what was going on.

- It didn't take long. I was bogged down in the mud of my methodology. It had worked wonderfully for a long time, but now it wasn't. I finally figured I had put my analysis in a box. I strictly adhered to development and structure equally. What I found was there are times price development needs to be given a greater weight than structure. However, in those cases more caution is warranted and risk analysis becomes more important.

- Proper Planning will give you the framework in which to make decisions. Imagine the trader or investor who straps into his chair in the morning, turns on the computer and gets ready for the markets to go up or down. He hopes to catch the trend a few times each day. He/she has set themselves up for failure.

- Consider another who spent the afternoon after the markets closed analyzing the price action from that day. He/she has determined what the trend is in various time frames. They know where areas of good trade location are. They make a plan that says if the market does this, I will enter short. If it does that, I will enter long. They know exactly what their risk will be and what is their expected return. Certainly, there are times when the market will throw a curve. That is the time to stand aside. The trader or investor who plans their trades will be much more successful.

- A trade plan should be developed for each day. Analyzing financial markets is a system of probability assessments. We take information that comes from the market and figure out the higher probability of one event occurring over another. We determine if the market is developing according to our plan. If it does not, we step back to see where we went wrong before we give the market our money.

- Proper planning will provide a method of review and control. Markets are always evolving. Our business must evolve with the markets. They are not static. Therefore, we cannot be static. This is why there is not a "holy grail" of investing. The "grail" doesn't exist because the markets are made up of humans. It is the participants behavior that determines where price will go. Information will come into the market and change that behavior, so we need to be aware the herd can change direction on a news event. We must, therefore, try to predict where the herd is going and whether it is getting ready to change direction or head over a cliff.

In summary, you will need to consider two types of plans. The first should be approaching your trading and investing as business. Therefore, it must be planned properly. The second is to plan your trades for each day. If you do both of these, no matter the time frame investor or trader you are, you will have increased your probability of success tremendously.

CHAPTER 2

THE BENEFITS OF PLANNING

WHEN I STARTED TRADING, I studied and applied many different methodologies and used many different technical indicators. Several years ago I was intrigued to find impressive information contained in a Market Profile™ chart. I read Peter Steidlmayer's book and began working with the charts and the information they provided. I was astounded at the amount of information the "profile charts" contained but was even more impressed with the way they incorporated all factors in the determination of value by a market. I found a "jewel". It is a method of analysis that is far superior to any other, at least for me.

As I progressed in my search to understand this methodology in more detail and apply it to my own trading, I also found there were other principles that were very important to the determination of success. Additionally, I worked with individual clients and corporate clients over the years. The result of that work has given me the ability to see and understand similar things that people consistently do that make them successful.

Steidlmayer, at the beginning of his book Steidlmayer On Markets, makes a statement that I have never forgotten. He states, "The most important element in becoming a successful trader is having a sound background consisting of a strong base of knowledge acquired from being active in the markets through time. Building this background is in some ways the easiest and in other ways the most difficult thing for a trader to accomplish. Trading experiences, observations of all kinds, a focus on what is most important, and a clear understanding of business principles are all necessary ingredients in a strong trading background. Awareness and patience are also required to further develop one's background. Without a sound background, one's trading cannot be consistently successful. With it, one can develop clear, correct ways of thinking and confidence in one's trading judgment. In today's fast moving world, some traders try to bypass the crucial first step of developing a sound background, and then rationalize the lack of background for the rest of their careers."

When I read the above, I thought of the different methodologies I had tried in trading. I too, sought the "holy grail" at one time. If there is a "holy grail", it is called hard work and attending the college of hard knocks and experiences. However, what I had come to realize was during that search, I was gaining knowledge and experience in the markets. I was a student of the markets. I paid a good price for it along the way but I made sure I learned from both my successes and failures.

Steidlmayer refers to building a background for the trader. Probably one of the most important statements he makes is to have a "clear understanding of business principles". If you have been in business before, then you know the business process begins with planning. Planning sets goals and objectives. Planning enables you to organize for success. It gives you the ability to determine how you will operate in the market you have chosen to enter. You will evaluate and understand your competitors and seek to look for opportunities, while at the same time trying to identify threats. More importantly, you will set a standard that will define success and failure. Defining success is extremely important. If you are not becoming successful, then you must take corrective action. Do not continue doing the same thing. Make well thought out and tested changes.

There is a psychological aspect of trading you will need to overcome. It is difficult, but once you overcome it, you will have taken a big step forward toward success. One psychological aspect is the feeling of a need to always be in a trade. I know, because I have experienced it and I still fight it. After all, if we are not in a trade, we are not making money. That feeling leads to forcing trades and taking more risk.

Denise Shull wrote a great book on the psychology of trading: Market Mind Games. In it she discusses feelings and emotions. Often, we are told to control our feelings and emotions. Denise discusses embracing them, not overcoming them. In the movie Top Gun, Maverick, played by Tom Cruise makes a statement: "I feel the need, the need for speed". As traders and investors we feel the need, the need to trade.

A good plan will hold you accountable and give you the parameters in which you can and cannot take a trade. I can't tell you how thankful I have been in the past when the need to trade has arisen but the discipline of holding to my plan saved me money. There are a few times when the trade would have worked out but the majority of them would have cost money.

One of the first times I spoke at a seminar I wondered how the individuals would feel about the material I had to cover. I was presenting a section on planning. They had come from all over the world in search of new information, a system, a technique, the "holy grail". I wondered if they would really hear what I was about to say, or would they quickly yawn and dream of the next purveyor of trading miracles. All traders look for some easy technique that will lead to quick fortunes. I wondered how they would respond when I explained to them what they sought did not exist. I was resolute in my belief that if they truly heard what I was about to say, it would change their careers. They were all professionals who managed their own money or that of others. They were all seeking knowledge of how to improve profits or how to succeed in an industry where most people fail. I checked their faces once more. Their eyes were on me in expectation. I took a breath and began.

I explained the importance of approaching trading and investing as a business, which included the preparation of a solid business plan for the business and a trade plan for each day. I stressed the development of a good analysis methodology coupled with proper planning, would give them exactly what they were looking for. But, it was not easy. It was going to take work. I took them through the planning process.

It was time for a break. As they left the room, I heard John, from New Zealand, comment to someone that he had built and sold two successful businesses in New Zealand and had prepared elaborate business plans for each. He said he had been trading for two years and it never occurred to him to prepare a business plan for his trading. He said with the methodology that I was teaching and the proper planning he had finally found a combination that would give him the success he had been in search of.

People all over the world enter into the business of trading and investing their own money every day. Most fail. From work I have done with clients over the years, I found that the ease of entry into the business, the lure of quick profits, and not approaching trading as a business leads most people to failure. The day trader and investor provide a necessary amount of liquidity to the financial markets. Unfortunately, they do not approach it understanding it is one of the most competitive businesses in the world. By structuring a sound business plan coupled with a methodology as an analysis tool, the individual investor can gain a competitive edge over the other 92% of those who fail.

As I stated previously, the business process is made of the following components: planning, organizing, managing and control. That is basically, the steps I will address in the coming chapters.

THE PLANNING PROCESS

The process to develop a sound plan will consist of several steps listed below.

- Develop a vision (A reason for entering the business of trading and investing)
- Set goals and objectives
- Adopt a methodology (Strategy)
- Assess strengths and weaknesses
- Analyze the environment of the financial markets
- Organize for success
- Develop an outline for a trade plan for each day, week, month
- Adopt a financial plan
- Prepare control reports
- Create an implementation plan

If you take the action outlined in this book, you will move yourself much farther down the road to success. More importantly, you will have put controls in place that will keep you from jumping into the markets blindfolded.

Some of the key benefits to planning are:

- It will give you a consciousness of your vision and whether you are achieving that vision. This provides the glue to keep you working, especially on a "bad" day. If you know where you want to go and you chart a course to get there, then you can hold yourself accountable if you are not achieving the intermediate steps toward success.

- It provides the trader discipline. Consider the individual who trades without a plan. Losses mount but no corrective action is taken because he/she feels the trading will turn around soon. Successful businesses do not continue actions that are unsuccessful. Excuses are easy to come by. Taking corrective actions are more difficult but will result in a higher probability of success.

- It will structure a framework to gage success or failure. Most traders, if you ask them to define their success, will respond that they want to make money. Of course, we all want to make money, but how much money and when? Those are the important questions. If you don't know how much, then how can you gage whether you are on your way to success or not? Every business takes small steps in the beginning. Track your small steps. When those are successful, you can begin taking larger steps.

- It will help in making decisions and risk assessment. Knowing how much to place in a trade is a key success variable. Knowing how much you will risk on the trade if it goes against you is an even more important variable. After all, if you enter a trade thinking it will go in your direction, how far will you let it go against you before you realize your analysis is wrong?

- It offers help in analyzing the threats and opportunities in the market place. What instruments will you be trading? Some instruments offer reduced risk but the return is also reduced. You should be able to evaluate the probability of success for trades. If you do this, you can then decide on how much of a threat the trade is to your capital or how much of an opportunity it may be.

- It will remind the trader that he/she must manage the trading business to be successful. I prepare a yearly budget for my trading. Then, I break it down into monthly objectives. As I trade during the month, I also know how much I need to make each week to achieve my monthly goals. I can track my success by day, week, and month. In this way, I know whether I am set to reach the goals I set for myself for that year. If I am not, I can take corrective action.

- Proper planning inspires confidence in the trader that he/she is trading as a professional and running a successful business. It is a great feeling to know you are on track to becoming successful. It is a psychological advantage to know you have made your objectives and while there may be another trade opportunity, you don't necessarily have to take it if the risk appears to be higher than you prefer.

- Planning provides a tool for proper capital formation, and capital preservation. Success breeds success. Capital can come from many different places. You can increase it from your personal savings. You can increase it through your profitability or you can increase it by having investors. Before doing any of those, you must first build a track record. That means you must find some success that is above alternative investments and the returns they produce.

- A quality plan provides the trader accountability. You will need to hold yourself accountable. As traders, we do not answer to anyone but ourselves. It is very easy to let ourselves off the hook. After a bad day of trading, we can get up, leave the computer, ignore the day and tell ourselves we will get it back tomorrow. Accountability makes us stay at the computer, review our actions and figure out what we did wrong. With that information we can then attack the next day with a good education, experience, and an attitude of discipline. I explain to traders a losing trade is payment for an education the market has given you. Don't ignore that education. Learn from it. After all, you paid for it.

Now it is time to begin the planning process. I suggest you keep a pad near you as you read through the next chapters. Hopefully, your thoughts will begin to progress and you will begin the planning process while still reading.

CHAPTER 3

DEVELOPING A DECISION PROCESS

"METHODOLOGY"

THERE ARE BASICALLY TWO areas that will need your attention. Those are: business decisions and trade decisions. Look at it this way. If you were starting a manufacturing business, you would decide on how to setup the business, the property, plant and equipment you will need, and the capital necessary to be successful. You would also project how much you expect to make from the business. Those are the same business decisions a trader or investor must make.

The second deals with how you will operate the business, or how you will make the product that will provide the income necessary to pay expenses and make your expected profit. For the trader and investor, this is the methodology. Methodology is the process you go through to analyze a market or an instrument to decide the probability of one event happening over another. Trade decisions include where you will enter, expected profit, risk tolerance and trade management. This is also strategy development.

As a result, you must first plan your business. Define your vision, goals and objectives. Then, plan how you will achieve those goals and objectives. The first is the business plan. The second is the methodology that will define your trade plan for each day.

In summary, you must consider the following:

- Define your business. You must define your vision, goals, objectives, control procedures, reports, etc.

- Decide on the proper tools you will need to be successful. Is your equipment up to date? What programs will you use? Have you planned for any contingencies, etc.? Anticipate the "what ifs", especially if you are in a trade and the market is moving fast.

- Develop a methodology. How will you analyze the markets and develop a strategy for approaching each day? Even if you are an intermediate to longer term investor, what happens each day in the markets will affect your business and your success. Developing a successful strategy will take time and will need to evolve as markets evolve and as your experience grows.

- Trade management. How will you execute and manage your positions? Many people bought stocks at the highs of 2000 and 2008. Those who bought in 2000 waited sixteen years to get their money back. Those who bought in 2008 waited eight years. There is no reason to watch your portfolio or trade get crushed and then hope and pray it comes back to break-even.

- Define success. You will need to decide on how to define success and failure. This is important. Too often I have seen clients not define success. Therefore, they don't know when to take corrective action. Or, they set the success bar so high and find it is impossible to achieve.

Each of the items above will take time to develop. As you build your knowledge and experience with equipment and programs, you will eventually find others that are better. After all, technology is always moving forward and looking for better solutions. We must constantly be seeking the tools that will give us a slightly better edge. Additionally, how you develop your strategy will change over time as well as your tactics. Markets are fluid. They change constantly. Therefore, we must be aware and change with those markets. There have been many who have held to a rigid trade methodology that worked perfectly. Later, they found that methodology was not producing the results it had in the past. This is because the markets are made up of humans and those humans have emotions. The emotions change with time and information. Therefore, we must be adaptive as well. Long Term Capital Management made billions with an algorithmic program, until the market changed and almost brought down the entire financial system.

You will find, if you prepare your plan properly, it will be constantly changing. As I write this, I have just made a radical change in the strategy I use. So far, the results are improved over what I was doing in the past. That is what any good business does. It seeks to improve performance all the time. Never allow yourself to become complacent. Always seek to improve, to learn and to achieve greater success.

Business Decisions

Since this book is about how to avoid failure in a very competitive business environment, most of it will be centered around decisions that you will need to make. For the most part, it will not include legal and accounting advice. You should seek advice from your own lawyer and accountant in that regard. What I will cover in detail is the process you will need to go through to setup a professional business plan that will help you in protecting your investment in the business and to gain the greatest possible return on investment. Additionally, I will spend some time on capital formation

Any business that is managed professionally, has a business plan. It basically explains the product to be produced (trades); the way in which the product is produced (methodology); the cost of that production (risk); and the expected profits to be generated (reward). By the time you finish this book, you should have a good understanding of how you want to begin planning your business and how to go about it. Even if you have been trading and investing for years, it is never too late to plan properly. This is true even for the part time investor who is still actively working in a career.

I have seen many traders and investors who have given up in the financial markets because they either lost money or could not make the return they though they could achieve. They plug along and finally one day reality hits them. The computer is turned off and they tell themselves they need to take some time and will come back later. Whenever I hear someone say that, I know immediately they blew up their capital account and need to go back to work to earn more. Why would you allow yourself to get to that point? If something you are doing is not working, stop doing it! The real question you have to ask yourself is: how do you know you are not achieving your goals, if you haven't defined success? And, if you have defined success and are not achieving it, would it not be prudent to stop what you are doing, reassess, and then take corrective action? Having a sound plan, assuming you follow it, will keep you from the grave yard of traders.

When I work with clients, the first question I ask them is to define success. The answer is typically, "I want to make money". That is not an answer. You must define success and in doing so, you have defined the warning signal to take corrective action. If someone asked to invest your money for you, would you not be interested in how much he/she thought they could make? It would be the first question I ask. If they don't produce the expected return, I would be talking to them and asking what is the problem.

TRADE DECISIONS

Financial markets are made up of human beings. It is the collective determination of value that drives price higher or lower. It is our job to asses the higher probability of which way price will go based on the collective assessment. Therefore, just as there are business decisions that must be made, trading and investing is a decision process also. It is a technique of analyzing probabilities. The market gives us information as to the determination of value by the participants. It is our job to gather that information, interpret it and then decide on the probability of one event occurring over another. Keep in mind, there are no certainties. Therefore, no matter how secure you feel in your analysis, there is always some probability you are wrong. When I enter a position, I am always looking for information from the market that would suggest the alternative is beginning to increase in its probability. This would then suggest my analysis was not correct and the alternative is in the process of occurring. I can then take corrective action.

Most people think, once they have made the decision to enter a trade, their job is complete. Actually, it is just beginning. The trade must be managed. With each tick, the market is giving us new information. That information must be processed and a decision to stay with the trade or exit must be made. How we manage our positions is extremely important. Many traders enter a market only to find they are wrong. They allow the losses to build. Then, they have to work extremely hard to earn back what the market has taken from them. Additionally, there are many times a trade can be entered and become profitable, only to eventually reverse and the trader sees those profits evaporate and turn into losses.

The beginning of any attempt to enter a financial market begins with how you will analyze the market. This is what I call methodology. Methodology is the decision process you go through in analyzing the information from the markets to get to a final decision of whether to enter the trade or not, and where you will enter the trade. The methodology is how you develop your strategy. It is the process you go through to analyze a market or an instrument. It is important to have a decision process that analyzes and builds a strategy, executes tactically and allows for trade management. That decision process is typically the same for all three events. It is important for the decision process to continue, especially after the trade is entered. With every tick of the market, it is sending the trader more information on what the participants are doing and the direction price is going. If trading on a longer time-frame then the decision process must be made on that time-frame. In other words, a day trader using a one minute chart for tactical entry will need to monitor the trade on a one minute basis. A trader or investor who enters based on an hourly chart will need to monitor the trade on an hourly basis. Those using daily charts will do the same using longer term charts.

The methodology you use to analyze markets must be processed and decisions made all of the time. The herd can change direction at times without any apparent reason. Markets couple and then decouple. What worked this year may not work next year. You must constantly be analyzing and testing your analysis techniques. They must adapt to the changing behavior of the participants in the market.

Most all people looking to enter the business of trading and investing look for the "holy grail". They feel there is some secret methodology out there that if applied to the markets will result in tremendous riches. There are many individuals who have come to riches through touting they have found the "holy grail". Having been involved in the markets for over thirty years, I can tell you I have looked for that "grail". When I found it, I realized it was right in front of me all the time. The "holy grail" of investing is: Plan properly and do the work. The more work you put into your planning and analysis, the greater your profits will be. Too often I see people come into this business not willing to put in the work before entering the market. They simply want to click the mouse, get into the action and watch the profits soar. It is a recipe for disaster.

Once again, I am reminded of Long Term Capital Management. In the late 90s this hedge fund invested in the spread on various global bond positions. The decisions were made by an algorithm that analyzed those spreads. What the algorithm could not predict was the changing behavior of bond investors. When it changed, it reacted the way it always did. The result was LTCM almost took the entire financial system down with them. We must change as the investing environment changes.

PLANNING DECISIONS

One of the key ingredients to successful business is not just to define the business, and plan for its success, but also to plan for what will make you different than your competitors. In the investment arena your competitors are the most fierce. Each time you enter a trade, there is someone on the other side of the trade who thinks you are wrong and is trying to take your money. Therefore, how we plan the business can give us an edge over the competition.

I am a pilot. One day I was flying with someone who had flown in the military. It was a beautiful day. The sky was crystal blue with not a cloud in sight. The air was smooth and the engines were purring nicely. We had been talking when the conversation subsided for a moment. All of a sudden, he looked at me and asked what I would do if I lost an engine. My heart skipped a beat.

Immediately, I checked the gages. I was sure he saw something I had missed. Everything was fine. I listened to the engines to see if I could hear something. There was nothing that I could see or hear, except my blood pressure that had just increased dramatically.

I looked at him and explained the engines were fine and asked what he was talking about. What he said, I have never forgotten.

"When you are flying along and everything is perfect, just as it is today; when the engines are purring nicely, just as they are now, that is when you need to be prepared for anything to happen. Always know what you will do if you suddenly lose an engine."

He let me take that in for a moment and then he said, "It is the same way in business. When the business is moving along nicely, everything seems to be working perfectly, that is when something will go wrong. Always anticipate what you will do if the unexpected happens". It was good advice that I have never forgotten.

Those were wise words that apply to the turbulent air of the financial markets. When you think the trade is going perfectly, when you think you have the market analyzed perfectly, that is when something will happen. That is when your decision process must be defined and kick in. I have been in trades that were moving nicely and then in an instant the market reversed. You can be sure of your analysis. The trade can be working in your favor and then everything can change in an instant.

One day I was trading a certain stock. I had developed my trade plan for the day and the specific instrument was included in the plan. I was waiting for it to trade into an area of good trade location. An alert was set, along with others included in the day's plan. I moved on and was working on something else. My system at this point was basically automated. Suddenly, the alert went off. I looked at the charts and recognized immediately the stock that had moved into a place where I could execute tactically. I watched patiently. The tactical setup occurred and I entered a long position. A stop was immediately set and I went back to work.

Periodically, I would glance at the charts to monitor all of my positions. Everything was moving as I expected. Now it was up to me to manage the trades. A few minutes later and my eyes moved quickly over the positions. It couldn't be! I jumped from my chair and started to pull up the recent entry I made on another charting program. It had to be a bad tick. The stock had jumped literally 15 Dollars in a matter of seconds. Checking another source, I found it was not a bad tick. The company had made an unexpected announcement and it was obviously positive.

Not only had the stock jumped 15 Dollars, it was still rising. More importantly, it had blown through the next level of resistance. I immediately moved my stop up to that resistance that was now support. I didn't want much of the move to deteriorate if the market decided it had overreacted. Needless to say, I watched carefully the rest of the day and exited the trade before the close with an extremely nice profit.

My point here is the unexpected happened. There was no warning. It could just as easily have been a negative announcement and the stock could have plummeted. Even though I had a stop, I could have been filled at a much lower price in a fast moving market. It was a good lesson on being prepared for the unexpected.

THE TRADE PLAN

This is where strategy comes into the planning process. Strategy is the process we develop that will guide the company to the successful completion of its goals. Tactics are the implementation of the strategy and how it is carried out. Many traders and investors ignore the strategy part and just want to go straight to tactics. This is the greatest mistake they can make.

I received a call one day from an individual who wanted me to train him. We talked for a while and it became clear what he was looking for. He wanted to know the "holy grail". He finally came out and said it. He asked me to just show him my tactical entries. I explained that tactical entries were useless if you didn't know where to execute them. I went on and said that I would not train him unless he agreed to development of a sound strategy first. After a while he finally agreed. Before doing so, I had to explain to him, if I only trained him in tactics, he would fail and I don't like my clients failing.

In trading most traders don't have a strategy. They have a tactical plan, but not a strategic plan. The strategic plan and the tactical plan combine to make the trade plan. The strategic plan defines what analysis you will use. Your analysis tells you if the market does this, I will do that. If the market does that, I will do this. Knowing where to enter a market is as important as how you enter the market. They go hand in hand. Many have entered a trade seeing a trend only to find the market reverse. Understanding where important support and resistance levels are is critical. Knowing the time-frame you are investing in and the next greater degree time-frame will save you much agony.

The Tactical plan on the other hand tells you how to enter, the trade size you will use, trade management and when to exit the trade. Most short term traders do not make money. The reason is they assume trading is easy. They look at a chart and see short term trends and feel it is simple to buy low and sell high, or sell high and buy low. When they begin making the trades, they have eliminated the process of understanding where the market is in terms of its price development and risk management.

If you have ever entered a trade only to have it immediately go against you, then you most likely are executing tactically without a sound strategy. As part of the strategy, you have to understand the development of price in multiple time-frames. Consider the investor who enters a trade based on what he sees in terms of price development in a particular time-frame. But, what he/she has not considered is what is occurring in the next larger degree of time. What the individual sees as a developing trend in one time-frame may simply be the completion of a counter-trend move in a larger degree of time. When that counter-trend move is complete, the main trend exerts itself and a large move in the opposite direction occurs. This is how many traders get "run over" in their trades.

Many traders feel the market knows when they enter. It is specifically aware when they enter, because as soon as they do the market reverses and they lose money. The market does not discriminate between participants. The difference is some have a plan and a decision process that tells them when there is a higher probability of success to enter and then how to manage the trade. The work for an investor comes in developing a strategy. The easy part is to click your mouse and enter a trade. This is why most traders and investors fail. They eliminate the most important part: developing a strategy.

A strategic plan is more of a macro perspective of where you want to go and how you expect to get there. From a strategic planning perspective most traders fail. They don't have a strategy. Most traders don't know how to execute tactically. It is well known that most let their losses run and cut their profits short. The development of a strategy tells you where there is good trade location.

If, in the world of traders, everyone is using a similar analysis for their strategic plan, and most traders fail, then what can we do as traders to plan strategically so we can execute a more successful plan? In other words, most traders do the same thing each and every day. They execute. They observe. They execute again. At the end of the week or month they hope their account statement has grown and not diminished. Some win and most fail.

However, there are many successful traders. What is the difference? What makes one person more successful than the others? It can be a lot of things: capital, emotions, psychology, analysis techniques, experience, etc.

If you treat trading as a business, then you will take your success to another level. You must ask yourself, if I have competitors, then how can I beat my competitors? What can I do that is different than everyone else is doing? What is it that will set me apart from everyone else?

From a strategic perspective, you should seek to find the answers for a plan that will separate you from the rest of the competition. Separating yourself means making decisions about your business, how you will organize it, develop it, manage it and operate it.

One of the most critical aspects of running any business, but more critical to the business of trading and investing, is keeping your decision process flowing all of the time. This means making decisions on organizing for success, deciding on what is success and what is failure, deciding on an analysis methodology, deciding on trade tactics and management, and on how you will observe your decisions in real time and then adapt to changing environments, changing markets and changing trades.

The successful trader or investor will plan properly and constantly look at their plan and revise it. They will review their analysis and revise it. Finally, they will analyze their trade tactics and improve on them. This means we must constantly observe our actions, orient to the changing environments, decide on courses of action and execute. This is true for the business as a whole and the trade.

CHAPTER 4

THE DECISION PROCESS

There is an important concept I have used over many years introduced by John Boyd, the famous fighter pilot who changed military tactics. He is credited with being the father of new military tactics and with producing a strategy that has made US fighter pilots the best and most competitive in the world. His strategies were used in the first Gulf War and are still being used and developed today in military circles. In a book entitled, Certain to Win, Chet Richards uses Boyd"s strategies and applies them to business.

Richards found one of the keys to the execution of a business strategy was the development of what Boyd calls OODA loops. Richards explains it in detail. OODA loops are a constant process of using a strategy and executing it consistently with timely tactics. OODA stands for:

- Observe (Gather and gain all of the information you can from every source.). This means gathering all of the information you can on the markets and instruments you will trade. Having a good understanding of the environment for the markets you trade is critical. Knowing when information may come into that market that can change the perception of value by participants is extremely important. Analyzing the development of price in multiple time-frames and then looking for areas of good trade location will lead to the next step. In other words, what is the environment for the market and instrument I plan to trade.

- Orient (Use all of the external and internal information you have gained to figure out where you are and how you may want to act.) These two steps outline a strategy. Once again, this is important to business planning and trade planning. In other words, now you know where you are in the markets, you have to decide on where to enter and in what direction. Some call this trend analysis. I refer to it as understanding price development. With this step you have completed a strategic analysis. The next steps are tactical in nature.

- Decide (Decide on the correct course of action or tactic from your observation and orientation.) In other words, absorb all of the information you can and then make a decision to act. This means you know if the market does this, you will do that. If the market does that, you will do this. When it does one of those events, you take a position.

- Act (Execute.) This means putting your business or trade plan into action. Click the mouse and enter the trade! Now you are committed.

The key to executing OODA loops is not to stop once you have gone through one. They are redundant. You immediately begin again and start observing the action of the instrument you entered. Each tick of the trade is sending you more information on what the market is going to do. You must interpret that information, decide and then act. A lot of times the act will be to stay with the position. Other times it will be to move your stop, or it could be to exit the trade. More importantly, as a trader and investor, your job will be to constantly interpret information coming from the market to determine if your strategy is working or not. If not, then you will have to adapt and change.

The same is true from a business management perspective. If you have set a goal to make X% return on capital and at the end of the month and you are not making it, you must observe, orient, decide to make a change, and then act on it. Remember, you have a plan. If you are not achieving the objectives in the plan, you have to analyze the problems, orient yourself to what occurred, decide on a change and then act on it. Once you do, the process starts over again. Proper business and trade planning is an ongoing process.

Many people would have saved a lot of money, if they only had a plan. The critical issue is the plan gives you a measuring stick. If you are not executing successfully, then stop, reassess what is happening and then take corrective action. There are still times now that I will stop trading because something is not working in the plan or I am not adapting to a changing environment. Once I orient myself again, I will begin the implementation phase.

Boyd found in his work as a military strategist that pilots who could execute OODA loops quicker were many times more successful in downing their opponent than pilots who could not execute them, or held to a strict tactic. The same is true with the trader and investor. If you take a position and then ignore it, you are gambling and putting your hard earned capital at risk. On the other hand, the investor who interprets information from the market faster, orients his strategy to that information and acts quickly will reduce risk and increase profits. So too will the investor who analyzes his performance pursuant to a business plan.

Therefore, in practice we have to consider two different OODA Loops. The first is the decision process of planning, organizing, managing and controlling our business of trading and investing. The second is the decision process of evaluating the trade or investment and then managing that trade. Remember, OODA Loops are dynamic, not static. Once you have completed the "Act", it is time to begin the reorientation and process and go through the loop. From the business management perspective, we have to assess and analyze performance on a daily basis.

OODA LOOPS AND TRADING

Consider the following scenario. You have analyzed a Stock or a Stock Index Future. You have identified the trend in at least two degrees of time and understand where the main trend is going. You have identified an area of good trade location. The market moves into that area and you are ready. You have just completed the Observe and Orient functions of the loop. You have defined a trade strategy. The instrument is strengthening in the direction of the trend.

Based on the above, you decide to enter the market. As part of that decision process, you know where you will enter and exactly where you will place your initial stop. This is the Decide part of the loop. Stop placement is critical to success. Your analysis tells you the stock is going higher. Where would the stock have to go to prove your analysis incorrect? That is a critical question that needs to be answered before you enter. Also, how much money are you willing to risk on the trade? You should know the answer to that as well. If the point of where the stock would go to prove your analysis wrong is in excess of the amount of money you want to risk, then you may not want to take the position. Or, you may decide to go through the Loop one more time and revise your decision before acting.

I was trading ten S&P futures contracts one day. My analysis told me if the market moved to a certain point that it was a buying opportunity. The market did exactly as I anticipated. However, when I looked at where the S&Ps could go to prove my strategy incorrect, it was more than my risk tolerance on any one trade would bear. Instead of passing on the trade, I lowered the number of contracts traded until the risk tolerance fell within my plan. Always know how much you are willing to risk on any one trade. That will dictate position size and risk tolerance. This is the importance of proper planning.

The next step is to act. This means clicking the mouse. It means committing your resources and risking capital to gain a fair return on that capital. Your decision process has brought you to the point that you have evaluated what you feel is a good reward to risk scenario. You have jumped in and your capital is now exposed to the changing market forces.

The trade is not over and neither is your decision process. Depending on the time-frame you are trading, you must continue to evaluate all of the information the market continues to give you. Assume you are trading the Stock Index Future in a short time-frame. This means that with every tick information is being given to you that will confirm or deny your strategy. If you are a long term investor, what happens each day is important for you to analyze.

Once in, you must begin a new decision loop. This starts with observing the market again. Is volume increasing in the direction of your move? If not, what could be happening? If the market does not move away from your entry quickly, what could be happening? You must continue to observe all information from the market. If volume is increasing and the market is moving in the direction of your trade, when and where will you move your stop? Proper trade management is part of the planning process. These are all things that should be well thought out and planned in advance.

The observation continues as you orient yourself to the new development of the market as it continues to extend. Then, you realize it is coming into another Key Reference Area and volume is falling off. You decide the trend is coming to an end and you move your stop to lock in additional profits. The act is moving the stop and realizing the profits you had thought would occur as a result of your initial strategy (observation and orientation).

I happened to be looking at a stock I felt was overpriced. It had moved off of its highs and was down significantly on the day I decided to trade it. I was concerned over the extent that it had moved already but it had consolidated. I felt if it broke to the downside of that rotation, there would be a decent move. Volume moving into the consolidation was very strong.

As I was observing and orienting myself to that particular stock, I noticed that it was approaching the lower extreme of the consolidation and volume was increasing, suggesting it was ready to breakout to the downside. I decided I would enter a short position and would place a stop just above the upper extreme of the consolidation. I acted and was filled immediately.

Within a few minutes, the stock had moved another few dollars lower and volume had increased substantially. I continued to observe and immediately moved the stop to break-even. The stock paused and started back up. At that point I had no risk in the trade but did not want to lose the substantial profits I had earned in a short time period. I observed the rotation back up was on much lower volume and decided I would stay with the trade.

A few minutes later the stock moved lower again on increasing volume. However, the volume did not increase as much as the volume on the breakout. This suggested the possibility sellers were exhausting themselves. From that orientation, I decided to move my stop down to the top of the previous bar on a five minute chart. A few minutes later I was stopped out for a nice profit. The stock then rotated back up and tested my entry point. Sellers were exhausted and buyers stepped in.

I spent about fifteen minutes observing and orienting myself to develop a strategy. The decision process and actual action took about another fifteen minutes. During that thirty minute period I was constantly running through the OODA loop process and making decisions on almost a tick by tick basis.

I have used this decision process in varying time-frames. If I trade a market on a thirty minute basis, then I am interested in the observation and orientation on a thirty minute time-frame, not so much a tick by tick basis. Therefore, you can use the OODA loop in varying time-frames.

Longer term investors should use the same process, except on longer time-frames. Those who have their money professionally managed should constantly be observing the performance of the manager. We no longer live in a time when you can invest for the long term. Certainly, using stops and getting out in major corrections can enhance profits tremendously.

OODA Loops and Business Planning

Business planning works in the same way as a trade plan. Once the plan is complete, the trade plan established and the analysis begins, it is important to execute the OODA loop for the business as a whole also.

If the trader finds the strategy and tactics are not working once executed, he/she begins the new OODA loop immediately and it tells them there is a problem. The new loop begins and, if necessary, changes are made to the entire plan through the planning process.

Execution of OODA loops takes place at all levels of the traders planning and execution of trades. At the end of the day, week and month the trade operations are observed; the observations are oriented with the changing environment and the plan expectations; decisions are made on how to correct actions to achieve goals or how to capitalize on positive results; action is then put into place to move the trade business along to a successful outcome.

Most important in the planning process (Observe and Orient) is to keep good records. It is those records that show the results of your strategy that become extremely important in the Observation phase. In other words, the records you keep in your trading business are the information you will need to complete future loops.

As a result, your use of the OODA loops becomes important to your success from two different perspectives.

- They help in developing and maintaining trades.

- They help in developing and maintaining a successful trading business.

It is important to remember when you take a loss in a trade or investment, you have just paid for an education. Look at what you did. Observe what the instrument did. Analyze the mistake and learn from it. Turn the loss into a benefit by using it as an education. Learn from your losses. Also, it is important to do the same thing with your successes. Analyze them and endeavor to continue performing to the same degree of success.

I set a strategy in the fund that I mange that will result in a minimum rate of return I feel is reasonable and achievable. I keep daily, weekly and monthly records. I use those records all the time to make decisions on what I do and how to change my actions. If I am behind my goals, then I have to re-orient myself, come up with a new business strategy and/or tactic and then execute again. In this way, I am holding myself accountable so my investors don't have to hold me accountable when they receive their quarterly reports. This is extremely important for any trader or investor, especially if you are managing your own money. I have seen many times losses taken and they are simply shrugged off by the trader. He mentally tells himself tomorrow will be better. Next month will be better, etc. You must hold yourself accountable. You must review your performance constantly and you must make changes if it is necessary. If you are reaching your goals and objectives, then recognize what you are doing that is making you successful and capitalize on it.

A few years ago the information coming into the market was not positive for stock prices. The economy was slowing down. Earnings were falling and unemployment was rising. Volume on each move higher was decreasing. On any move to the downside volume was increasing. The environment for rising prices was decreasing rapidly. I was certain a substantial correction was in the near future. I knew my analysis was correct. I began building short positions. Once the correction came, I would make an incredible return. I was set.

Day after day, week after week, small corrections would occur but then stocks would move to slight new highs. This happened over and over. Bad news coming into the market seemed to be good for stock prices. Finally, after putting up a dismal performance, my business plan made me step back and reorient myself. I exited all but a small short position and then stood back from the market. My orientation was wrong. I was interpreting information incorrectly. But, that seemed impossible. Everything I knew, everything that had moved the markets before was screaming "sell".

What kept me from entering again was a sound plan that made me continue analyzing until I was back in sync with the market participants. What I eventually found was the behavior of the participants in stocks had changed. They were no longer focused on fundamentals or the environment. What they were now focused on was easy money policy and low interest rates from the Federal Reserve. Everything they and I knew from the past had been thrown out the door. My experience from the past was keeping me from making profits. The behavior of market participants had changed. I needed to change as well.

In order to adapt, I had to change my thought process and observe and orient myself to a new behavior by market participants. To do this I needed a new discipline. By adhering to my business plan, I was able to step back from the markets and stop fighting them. It was only because I was managing the business according to a plan that I had to reassess, not just my trading, but my complete analysis techniques. Without a business plan that told me I was not achieving success, I may not have stopped and stepped back to reassess before significant losses were experienced.

The key to successful trading is therefore doing things that other traders are not, and executing the decision process on a faster basis than your competition. If you find that your actions as a trader or investor are not producing the profits you planned, then you must take alternative action. I cannot stress strongly enough that evaluating yourself and your results is critical to success. The traders who I have seen fail, do not keep good records. They do not evaluate themselves, nor do they change their behavior. They lose money and then come back the next day doing the same things that lost them money the day before. The only thing that has changed is the mental game they play with themselves. Remember: the "holy grail" of trading and investing is in doing the work and adapting as the behavior of participants change.

When most have had enough of losses, they do one of two things. They either look for a new system, blaming the losses on a failed system and guru who sold it to them or they simply move on to a different business. The former typically will repeat the failure process. The latter will generally never come back to trading and investing.

Assume a trade is not working out, you are stopped out or you pull the plug on the trade......hopefully! You then evaluate what happened and try to see what mistakes you made. You learn from your actions and execute differently next time. The same is true with your business. If it is not working out, pull the plug. Stop trading! Evaluate where the problem may be and then begin again. Change what you did in the past that did not lead you to success.

This decision process goes on as long as you are in business and as long as you are trading and investing. The important aspect is to define success. Success in your money management business and success in each individual trade.

If you are a longer term investor, don't just leave your money to the whim of the market. What would you define as success? What return on capital is successful to you? Once defined, you can track your success and make changes as necessary, instead of being at the mercy of the markets. If you have money that is being managed by a professional manager, what is the expected return? You must know it, because if he/she is not producing, you should look for another manager.

I met with an investor who had millions invested in the markets. Most of his money was being managed by one of the larger wall street firms. As we were discussing his investment with me, he boldly stated that he had just moved several million dollars from one wall street firm to another. I asked him why and he said they had not met his minimum objectives for return.

I questioned him on his expectations. His response was simple. If he invested in an index fund, he would not have to pay fees to a manager. Therefore, his minimum return to keep his capital was the performance of a specific index fund, plus the manager's fees, and a percentage in excess of the index. If the manager could not keep up with the index, cover his fees and give him a return greater than the index, he was wasting his time and money on that manager. He had a well-defined plan and held the managers accountable for it.

If you are managing your own money or trading and investing for yourself, you must hold yourself accountable and that means deciding on what is success and what is failure. You must review your performance constantly and make appropriate changes. There are times when you, as the shareholder, will need to take the trader to the wood shed and have a moment of truth. Other times you will send the trader on a well-deserved vacation or take him/her out to a great dinner.

CHAPTER 5

REALIZING YOUR VISION

T HERE ARE A LOT of things you can do with your life, but if they don't bring you to fulfilling your vision, why do them? If you are not achieving your vision for your life now, then change it. If trading and investing are not fulfilling your life's vision, change. If you are not successful, figure out why and develop a course of action that will bring you to success. If you are in business, why? What is the purpose of the business? What dreams will it fulfill for you? The business is a vehicle that is taking you to some distant goal.

When I started in business, I was aggressive. I wanted to succeed financially. I worked hard. I had a wife, four children, a large house, two airplanes, expensive cars and lots of other toys. One day I realized they meant nothing. I arrived home from a trip and was met with four little children who rushed into their father's arms. It was then I understood. God had entrusted to me the lives of four precious children. I was giving them everything, except myself. A radical change was about to take place.

I was on my way to Atlanta to meet with my best friend from college. We had worked together for a couple of years after graduating, but he moved on to buy and build another business. Several years later, he sold the business and made a substantial amount of money. Life and business had treated him well.

For my part, I was in the process of looking to change directions professionally. Years of travel doing venture capital deals found me with more desire to spend time with my family, instead of making more money. The final act came when I spent nine months working on a workout of a hotel company in the mid-west. Much travel was demanded by the workout. I would return home on weekends realizing how much I missed my family.

My friend invited me to Atlanta to meet with him with the idea of starting a new business together. He wouldn't say much about it. I knew he had rented an office and was in the formation process.

Over the next three days, Alex explained a vision he had for an investment business that would initially trade futures and then move into equities. He laid out the steps for us putting in the initial capital, expected returns, costs, and his vision for the business at the end of five years. He showed me his track record to date, his methodology and outlined a complete business plan. He finished by asking me to move to Atlanta and be his partner.

The presentation was excellent. His vision included a minimum number of employees, substantial profits, the ability to travel and most of, all to be able to take time with family, which is what I wanted. He outlined the possibility of overcoming financial downturns by exiting long positions and entering short. In those three days, he had outlined for me a vision of a company that gave prestige, financial gain and the ability to spend time with my family. His vision became mine. Having built and managed a fairly large company, I was looking for something with less baggage.

After some negotiating, we came to an agreement. However, I was not going to move to Atlanta right away. We were in the process of selling our house and were looking for a new place to go, but I didn't feel going to Atlanta was a move I wanted to make right away. We decided to work together but in separate places. He stayed in Atlanta and I moved to the mountains of North Carolina for some much needed time with family.

I subscribed to real-time charting program and bought a new computer system. Alex had the same installed in the office in Atlanta. We funded the brokerage account and collaborated on our analysis and decisions. Over the next several years, we studied together, went to seminars, read books and did everything we could to gain an edge over the competition. We both were fierce competitors and failure would not be tolerated.

Since that time, the vision we both adopted has never left me. In fact, it has led me to be able to work from home or wherever I wanted. I have taught and spoken at seminars. I have helped other individuals develop their own trade and investment businesses, written articles, and started and operated two small hedge funds. In all I endeavor, it is the vision that keeps me going. It is the vision that is the glue that holds me to the path I chose all those years ago. It is vision which has brought me to writing this book.

Let me be very clear. It may sound as if our decision to enter the trade and investment business was easy and well rewarded.

Trust me. It was not. There were many days, weeks and months we wondered how we would pay our bills. We learned two things along the way. The first was the importance of fulfilling our vision, and the determination to avoid the alternative. The second was our intent to learn from every trade.

My vision of being financially successful and being with family kept me going through the difficult times. Without that vision, I would have certainly given up, as most traders and investors do.

THE FIRST STEP

The first step in creating a vision is to dream. You obviously made the decision to enter the business because you are reading this book. If that is the case, then what do you want? Why are you entering this arena? The answer to these questions will be important. They should not be quantifiable. As I explained above, what drove me in the beginning was spending more time with my family. I had a desire to be more a part of their lives. I wanted to be at the soccer games. I dreamed of skiing with them and hiking the Appalachian Trail. I wanted to be there for dinner every night. I also wanted to provide a certain standard of living for them. In summary, I wanted time with family and money. I sought the gratification of being a successful investor and looked forward to being the captain of my ship with no demands made by employees or other companies. What I made, I wanted to keep. I saw myself as a professional who could rise in a field of financial giants. My vision included being a professional, financially successful and involved in the lives of my family. None of that is quantifiable. It was simply a picture of what I wanted my life to look like.

Over the years, I've had job opportunities and been given other venture opportunities. When sifted through the prism of my vision, if they didn't meet that vision, I let them go. Therefore, as the first step of your planning, I urge you to take some time and dream. What is it you want? More importantly, what do you feel is your life's purpose. I asked one client that question. He thought for a moment, looked me in the eye and explained that he had a charity he loved and worked with. He wanted to make enough money to support himself and donate to the charity. That was his vision.

I was fortunate to have a wife who wanted her husband home and didn't care that much about "things". I came to a conclusion on my trip to Atlanta. I realized my vision over twenty-five years ago. I still pursue it every day. I will not let it go. It is the glue that holds my professional career together. It holds my life together. It is my purpose. So, the first step is to take as much time as necessary and find your vision. Write it down. It should not be quantifiable. That will come later. Describe the life that you want to lead. What is it you really want to do? What is the purpose of your life? Once you find it, never let it go. Never accept failure. Realize it will take hard work and commitment.

In addition to the above, it is perfectly appropriate for you to be in the process of planning your business while you are studying methodologies, analyzing markets and educating yourself. I do caution against taking any tactical steps until you have completed the planning process and have developed sound strategy and tactics. Test the strategy and tactics before entering the markets, if you are just beginning.

The vision statement is the reason you are entering the business of trading and investing. Ask yourself why. Why are you going into this business? Take your time in answering. It is the most important question you will ask yourself in developing a successful plan. Everyone has a different vision for themselves. Mine is likely different than yours. In a few sentences write yours.

I like to think of the vision statement as the glue that holds the business and the plan together. Most successful people have a vision of themselves doing something or being somebody. They see where they want to go and design a plan on how to get there. However, when things get dark or failure seems to loom in the distance, it is the vision that energizes. The vision makes you get up, dust yourself off, and begin again. I refused to accept failure because I wanted my vision more than failure. When a lack of success loomed, and there were many failures. I fought hard against it.

It is the vision you have for yourself that will help you overcome all odds, all hurdles and all those who tell you success is not achievable. It is the purpose you have embarked down this path. Remember, it is unquantifiable. Goals are quantifiable. They will come next.

I work with some retired individuals. Their vision is to manage their own money successfully, to achieve personal and financial satisfaction from the study and analysis of financial markets and to have the freedom to travel, spend time with family and still run a professional business.

When I started the Venture Capital firm early in my career, it took off with great success. It seemed I had a golden touch. With each success came more and more capital. However, then I hit a wall. A deal lost money. No matter how hard I worked or what I did, it was not going to recover. I felt terrible. The investors were going to lose money. I felt as if I had let the whole world down.

Then, I remembered my vision. I saw myself as the professional I had worked and studied to be. I remembered the reason I entered the business and had to admit there are going to be some losses. I made the decision that a loss will not keep me from my vision. I cut the loss, notified the investors, dusted myself off and started once again.

Venture capital is a lot like trading and investing. You make a lot of money on trades and then a loss hits you that you didn't expect. That is the time when you feel the worst and you think success is not for you in this profession. Successful traders will keep the vision in front of them for dark days. The vision is the light you will search for when things are not going the way you expected.

I ask my clients to take time to dream. What is your dream for entering this profession? I know you want to make money, but why do you want to make money. How do you see yourself a year from now, ten years from now? What would you like to be able to do?

I am finding more and more people who want to manage their own money. They don't want to throw "caution to the wind" by allowing someone else to make decisions for them. As a result, they are beginning to understand the need for a well-developed and thought out business plan that begins with the vision statement.

I have a friend whose father is in his 90s. He trades options! When I asked him why he was trading options, he said, "I want to keep my mind sharp and active. I want to analyze and compete in business. I want to feel as if I am still doing something". For him, his vision is not to be retired but to be active and involved in a profession. He gets up every morning and sees himself analyzing and studying the markets and making professional decisions.

The Second Step

Your second step is to decide on how to achieve your vision. The deeper you go in search of your true vision, the easier it will be to move forward with the second step. It will save you from walking down several paths you later find are not producing the fruits you thought.

Your vision is really your purpose in life. For me, the pursuit of building a large company was not it. When I realized that, I started searching and finally found what I was looking for. Once found, I was able to devise a strategy to take me where I wanted to go. I never let go of that vision. There were setbacks, hurdles, problems and many days and nights of wondering if I was on the wrong path. One thing never failed. I knew what I wanted. I knew the life I wanted to lead and I sought it out.

The doctor I ran into at the soccer field, had a vision for his life and decided medical school was the way to achieve that vision. Later, he decided he could achieve that vision by getting in the business of investing.

I assume trading is the vehicle you have chosen to achieve your vision. Whether it is to gain a better return on your capital, give you freedom to work for yourself, the satisfaction of competing in financial markets, or just something to keep you active and busy, there is a vision of what you want to accomplish. You need to seek that vision and write it down.

If you study any successful individual, especially entrepreneurs and investment professionals, they all had a vision of what they wanted to accomplish. They pursued it with vigor. They made mistakes and they learned from those mistakes. They fell, but then got back up, brushed themselves off and started again. There was no hurdle too high, no valley too deep, and no amount of failure that would keep them from achieving success. That is the way it must be in the business of trading and investing.

There will be days when you will truly believe the markets are intent on destroying you. You will feel depression and just about every other emotion there is. It will be important to learn from the successes and failures. Never let an educational opportunity pass. Don't be afraid to admit you made a mistake and learn from it. And most of all, always be humble. Even when you make a killing in a trade, be humble. If you are not, the markets always find a way of giving you the humility you need. A few good trades do not make a trader or a financial genius. It is the long term performance in which we have to judge ourselves. That performance must have an objective. The objective is the delivery of our vision.

Once you start down the path of seeking your vision using the vehicle of trading and investing, you will meet with stiff challenges. In fact, you may even get to the point that you wonder if it is possible at all to achieve success. It is how you overcome the challenges that will give you success or deal you a final blow of defeat.

I recently read one of the best books I have ever come across. Steven Pressfield wrote: The War of Art. At the beginning of the book Pressfield writes, "If you believe in God (and I do) you must declare resistance evil, for it prevents us from achieving the life God intended when He endowed each of us with our own unique genius. Genius is a Latin word; the Romans used it to denote an inner spirit, holy and inviolable, which watches over us, guiding us to our calling". As someone who has been active in the markets for many years, "resistance" will come. "Resistance" is anything that will hinder or stop you from achieving your vision. We must always fight back against "resistance" with all of our might. Not to, means defeat. Resistance will tell you not to do the analysis. Resistance will lead you to blindly enter the markets without doing the work. Resistance will lead you to believe you are smarter than everyone else. Resistance will have you believe there is a "holy grail" to investing. Resistance says, "It is easy". Resistance makes you feel you MUST trade, even when your strategy says differently.

So, if you have chosen this business to take you to your vision, you will meet with stiff resistance. Trust me. I have experienced it and still experience it. How you deal with the resistance will make the difference between success and failure. Remember, it is your vision that is the glue that will keep you going when all seems lost. It is the vision that will get you up in the morning to study, or keep you up late into the night preparing for the next day. It is the vision that will give you the fuel to go on.

So, what is your dream? What is the purpose behind your desire to be successful as a trader/investor?

CHAPTER 6

ESTABLISHING GOALS

NLIKE THE VISION STATEMENT, the goal statement is quantifiable. This is the road map that will take you to your vision. Some business plans are developed over a ten year basis. In other words, they look out ten years and project where the business will be at that time. In the investment business things can change quickly. New instruments are invented. Derivatives on new products come into the market. Regulations change. Companies rise and fall. More importantly, the environment for the financial markets change. This is probably the most important. Opportunities in one market may decline while they increase in another. Therefore, I suggest looking out three years for planning purposes. There are some who may want to look out five, but even then it is stretching the time-frame.

Once you have completed the vision statement, the fun begins. Working on goals is specific in nature and should be measurable. It is here that you will determine your success or failure. This is where you take the picture of your vision and begin to paint it on the canvas. You begin by picking out the colors and deciding on which brush strokes come first and which will come after.

Goals are specific. They are not just financial, but we are going into this business to make money. So, how much do you want to make and when? Be realistic.

With the vision statement now complete, we have a picture of the life we want to have. The goal statement tells you how much of the picture will be complete and in what time-frame. Remember, it is a process of achieving a goal. It may not necessarily be accomplished in one year. My doctor friend, I discussed earlier, was setting up his business as a second profession that would eventually become his main profession. That could take five to ten years depending on his vision and goals.

So, the question to begin with is, where do you want to be in three years in achieving your vision? Realism is important here. In reality, to achieve your vision it may take ten or twenty years, or you may be able to achieve it in three. The important part is to look down the road three years and decide how far you want to have traveled.

In my case, I knew my vision. It meant I had to figure a way to earn a living and not be tied to an office or an office chair. When I left the office, I didn't want to worry about the business. I wanted to be able to close the door and know that nothing could happen until I returned. More importantly, I wanted to know that all the money I made, I would be able to keep and not have to pay employees. Time with family was my ultimate vision.

What does your vision mean to you in quantifiable terms? In others, If your vision is to be able to make enough to leave your current profession, to purchase a second home, or whatever it may be, bring it down to a quantifiable term. How much money would you have to have to achieve your vision? If your vision will take more than three years in realistic terms, what progress do you want to make toward that vision at the end of the three year period?

THREE YEAR GOALS

I will call him Mike. That wasn't his name but he was from Europe. He traveled to the United States to spend a week with me. He had paid a lot of money to be mentored and in travel expenses. During the week, we would work on writing his business plan and trading the markets. I would attempt to teach him all that I could about the analysis, implementation and management of managing his own money. More importantly, we established the foundation for a sound business plan.

Typically, in the mornings I spend time with clients teaching them what I know about analyzing the markets, preparing the trade plan, executing tactically and trade management. In the afternoons we spend time working on the business plan and if there is a trade in progress, we manage it.

On the afternoon of the second day, Mike and I started on goals. I asked him where he wanted to be in terms of money at the end of three years. "300% per year return on capital," he stated proudly. A smile crossed his face. Our eyes met and I realized he was serious. He looked to me for approval of that goal. I knew I had an uphill battle.

"Mike, if you can make 300% per year, why would you trade your own money? If you can do that, there are hedge funds and banks that will pay you millions a year to do it for them and you don't have to risk your capital." The smile left and his eyes blurred over. I tried to explain, while there may be a few here and there who can make 300% periodically, the realistic chances of doing it are slim. His goal, as a new trader, was unrealistic. He expected to make 100% the first year; 200% the second year; and 300% every year after that. He was setting himself up for failure. Either he would fall short of his goal, or he would have to take high risk trades and the probability of success would diminish with the greater risk. It is important to recognize the higher the expected return, the higher the risk.

One of the most difficult concepts for me to get clients to understand is risk management. The psychology of wanting to make "big bucks" is too great. Therefore, their positions size is too large and there is no risk control.

I suggest beginning with a percentage, on an amount of capital. After all, if your capital is small, it will take a longer period of time to get up to where you want to be financially. On the other hand, if you have a larger capital account, it will not take as long. What is important here is what return on capital you are looking for. Be reasonable. Do not set yourself up for failure. Rather, position for success initially. You can always change your goals at any time. In fact, you will find it necessary to revise your plan periodically.

Important to your decision process is whether you will take both long and short positions. If you will only consider long positions, whether it be in stocks, bonds, or futures, then you can set your goal to meet a benchmark, such as the S&P 500 Index. Or, you can set the goal to the Index plus a certain percentage. In this case it would be the S&P 500 Index plus 10%.

The problem with this is you will be allowing opportunities to pass you by. There are many market corrections where lots of money can be made. If you only consider long positions and there is a 20% correction in the market, then you have gone a period of time by keeping up with the Index but you have lost money. It is important to keep focused on the fact that you are running a business. Therefore, the business must have revenues to survive in both rising and falling markets.

Let's take a hypothetical example to go through the process. I will assume you have a beginning capital account of $25,000. Using the process of planning from now to the third year, you may assume you can make a 30% return per year. This means at the end of the first year you will have $32,500 in capital and will have made $7,500 for the year. This is only $145.00 per week or an average return of about $29.00 per day.

The second year your beginning capital is $32,500 but you feel a 40% return on capital is reasonable considering the experience you have gained. Therefore, at the end of the second year you will have a capital account of $45,500 and will have made $13,000 for the year. Your average daily profit will have been $55.00.

Once again, the third year begins and you start with $45,500 in capital and you again feel you can up your percentage to 50%. At the end of the third year your capital account will be $68,250 and your annual profit is $22,750. You average daily profit will need to be $95.00.

While a 40% to 50% return would be stellar, my point is to show what it takes on a daily basis to achieve incredible returns. There is no reason to put your money at risk unless your analysis tells you there is a high probability for that trade to succeed.

Another person my decide they want to have $5,000 of income per month. This is $60,000 per year. They feel a reasonable return would be 30%. Therefore, they would need $200,000 of capital and would need to average about $250 per day. I should mention, there is nothing wrong with planning to accumulate $200,000 in capital first and then implement the business plan.

When you break these goals down into shorter time-frames, you can see how the daily objectives are easy to achieve. This will result in a more conservative risk tolerance, fewer losses and preservation of capital and you can calculate position size appropriately.

I should mention that I picked a 30% return on a random basis. On the other hand, if you have a $25,000 account and want to make $75,000 per year, that is a 200% return. Unrealistic! You have to modify your goals and time-frame or figure a way to get more capital and bring the return percentage down.

Two Year Goals

Two year goals should be annual and not broken down monthly. Take into consideration increased knowledge, experience, success, return and risk.

One Year Goals

One year goals are specific. They should be broken down into yearly, monthly and weekly goals. I like to know what my daily goal is. At the end of each day, I chart my progress toward achieving my weekly goals. Those then tell me if I am meeting my monthly objectives.

There are times when I see that I am falling behind. When that occurs, I have to take corrective action. Other times, I will be ahead. If I want to take the day off, I will do it, or I will not trade until I see a very high probability of success in a position. When I am ahead, I will keep trading, but I defend my profits with every once of ability I have. Psychologically for me, the worst situation is to be ahead of my goals and then watch them disappear because of poor risk tolerance.

SIZE DOESN'T MATTER UNTIL IT DOES

I want to make a very important point here. Size does not matter! It only matters if you are looking at the dollars. What matters most is Return on Capital (ROC). I have gone through this with many clients in the past. Size is only a function of zeros and risk. ROC is a function of success. The person who makes a 15% ROC on a $300,000 capital account is no more successful than the one who makes the same return on a $5,000 account. It only matters when the position size results in too much risk and lower probability trades.

I have clients with little experience in trading and investing come in and want to trade futures contracts or large position sizes in equities. Their mindset is on becoming extremely wealthy by simply clicking a mouse button to get in and out of trades. What I try to explain to them is there is a relationship, not just between reward and risk but also between risk and experience. If you have little experience, then you have greater risk. This is a competitive business. You will not make money unless you take someone else's. That person is also trying to take your money. There is much to learn in this business and there is a cost to the education. Not every trade will be profitable and it will be important to learn from every trade: the losers and winners both.

Therefore, who is more successful? The person who makes a 20% return trading 10 shares of an equity or 1 futures contract, or the guy who barely breaks even trading 1000 share lots or 10 futures contracts? If you have gained the knowledge and experience to successfully trade 10 shares or 1 contract, then you can successfully increase your trade size by adding a zero. Nothing should change other than the zero. Your analysis stays the same. Your strategy has not changed. Your tactical entries and trade management are consistent. The only change is the addition of a zero to your trade size based on your experience.

Once you have been consistent with the first zero and your capital account has grown, add another zero. This is a concept of compounding on trade size based on your personal risk assessment and experience. If you are consistent doing one thing and your capital account allows it, there is no reason not to increase your size. What matters the most is consistency. It is not about size. It is about consistent ROC, then size can increase.

There are lots of books written about the psychology of trading and investing and a lot of discussion over the psychological aspects of trading large blocks of instruments. The only psychological problems you should have in trading large blocks of an instrument is if you are not consistent with your ROC. If ROC is not consistent, you may be putting your capital account in jeopardy.

Take two traders. One has a $5,000 account. The other has a $50,000 account. They both have a goal of making a 30% return. The position size for the smaller account will be much smaller than the larger one. However, the smaller account may start trading 10 shares of an equity, while the larger 100 shares. As success is achieved. One may decide to trade 20 shares and the other 200. It is risk management and consistency that matters.

My advice is, if you are just beginning or if you have not had great success in the past, start small. Take as much risk out of the business as you can. If you can make a 10% return on 10 shares, congratulations! Do it consistently, then increase your size. When you get up to trading 1000 share lots and want to jump to the futures markets, be my guest. However, if you do not have a stellar ROC record or are just beginning, you are putting your capital at great risk trying to trade large blocks or going into futures.

Another way to look at it is if you have a $25,000 account and expect to make a 30% ROC, then you expect to produce $$7,500 at the end of the year. This breaks down to about $30 per day. If you trade 10 shares of a stock, you need to see a $3.00 move. If you trade 25 shares, you need to see a $1.20 move in the stock. With 50 shares, you need a $0.60 move in the stock. 100 shares needs only a $0.30 move in the stock.

I hope you are seeing the theory here. Risk management, ROC and position sizing are all mathematically related. When a client asks me what size position they should be trading, the calculations are easy to start.

Monthly Goals

Ever since I started my own venture capital firm, I have always drafted business plans and have reviewed those plans against performance carefully. For me, the period of Thanksgiving through the end of the year is a planning time. It is during this time that I review my performance, make changes and then revise my longer-term plan.

In the first year of planning we break down the one year goals into twelve monthly goals. At the end of the first year, we review the performance, make changes and revise the plan. This means we look out another year as the third year and set those goals. Our second year goals are now our first year goals. If they need to be revised based on the one year performance, then revise them. Finally, the second year is now the current year so it needs to be broken down into twelve monthly goals. I have found this time period to be most rewarding. Even if I have not achieved my one year goals, I am able to plan corrective action.

When I had my company and we were in the process of raising capital for a deal, I knew exactly when the capital had to be raised and I knew how much. Based on that, I knew exactly how much time I had to raise the money and I could break it down into monthly, weekly and daily goals. I could keep up with our performance and make adjustments as necessary. You should manage your investment business the same way.

It would have been reckless of me to set a goal of raising a certain amount of capital in a specific time period and then not look at whether we were going to get there or not. I wanted to know the progress so I could make adjustments to insure success.

It is the same way in trading and investing. You should keep a record of each day. The daily tallies are not as important to me as the weekly. The weeklies get me closer to the monthly goals and the monthly goals get me closer to my yearly goals. If I miss my weekly goal, I know it is coming because I see what is happening each day. I can then try to correct before the week is over. If I miss my weekly goal, I have to try to correct before the month is over. Finally, if I miss a month, I know I have some work to do in the coming months.

WEEKLY GOALS

Now, break down your goals into weekly goals. Above, I talked about setting daily goals. They are not as important. There will be some days when you will not trade. Someone once told me trading is being long. Trading is being short. Trading is standing aside. I can tell you probably the most important of those three is knowing when to stand aside. I, along with many others, have been chopped to death trying to trade a market that is stalled or in a consolidation.

Important will be what happens on Friday night when you prepare control reports. What were the results of the week? Maybe you only got one trade off during the week and it made your weekly goal. Perhaps you traded fifteen times and didn't quite make your weekly goal. Or worse, suppose you traded and lost money for the week. This is extremely important. You must do the work to plot your progress and review your performance at a minimum on a weekly basis. I review my performance each day. I want to remember what I did that produced the profit, or I want to figure out what I missed that caused me to lose money. If it was a loser, then I want the education I paid for. The only way to get that is to and analyze performance.

Think of it this way. If you were running a manufacturing business and you had a certain amount of product you had to get out by the end of each month. Would you ignore the progress during the month and only hope and pray the product was made on time? Of course not. You would monitor performance on a daily and weekly basis. If production was falling behind, you would figure out what course of action you had to take to correct the situation and get back on course.

The psychology of many people coming into this business is to think they will hit it big with almost every trade. They lose a few but that big one is just around the corner and will erase all of the losses. The big ones are out there but they are not random. You can see them coming. This is a business of inches. It is a business of making a little here and a little there. It is a profession of managing risk so as not to give up profits or capital. It is accomplishing a specific goal by clawing our way each day to reach that goal. Eventually, we will hit the home run. Most important is to try to get on base every day.

OTHER GOALS

Probably the most important goals you should set are economic. After all, if you don't eventually make money, you won't be in business long. But, there are other very important goals to reach along the way.

EDUCATION

SEMINARS

Educating yourself is extremely important. I suggest attending a minimum of one seminar or convention per year. I have spoken and taught at many seminars and have found that even I can learn something new from the participants. There is always someone who has an idea, a concept or is searching for a new methodology to match the changing economic environment. Meeting and talking with other individuals is a tremendous way to make new business friends and learn much from their endeavors.

Many companies also offer webinars. In these you don't have to leave home. You can attend the seminar online. I have presented at several webinars and while the personal interaction is missing, which I feel is important, there is still much gained and at a much lower cost as a result of a lack of facility cost and travel related costs.

CONVENTIONS

These are another way of gaining a great education. A lot of times they will have exhibits of companies offering new products that can help with screening and analysis. I typically spend time talking to some of the exhibitors about their products. Some are not very good but others can be very thought provoking. Also, the classes that are offered can be very informative. Choose those classes wisely, as there are some speakers who are great speakers but I doubt they have really gained success in trading.

There is a wide variety of books and courses available to the active trader and investor. To choose, you must first decide on your feelings toward economic conditions. The person who feels investing for the long term is the way to go will look for books on how to pick stocks for the long term. Another who feels they don't want to sit through major market corrections will look for something different. Finally, the active trader and investor will find something more along the lines of how to analyze financial instruments in the short term.

There are also courses available. You can purchase these from various companies. The material will arrive and allow you to work at your own pace, submit questions and in some cases have a personal one on one session with the professional online. I have used this technique many times with clients.

MENTORING

Mentoring usually involves multiple personal sessions with a professional trainer. I have mentored many people and have enjoyed it greatly. Sessions can be held online or at the office of the professional. I have done both. Honestly, my preference is for the client to come to my office. We can get to know each other, work all day for several days and get much accomplished. We work through analysis, developing a trade plan for each day, establishing a business plan, assessing risk, trade management and tactical entries and exits, along with many other aspects of the business.

You must feel comfortable with the professional mentor. I suggest spending time talking to him/her on the phone or online.

Discuss exactly what you are looking for from the mentoring process and then evaluate the answers. The mentor will be your coach. They will be responsible for training you for competition. Therefore, you should feel comfortable with them and their ability to guide you and give you the education you are looking for.

I do have one warning about online mentoring. Don't waste your time and money or the professional's time if you are not serious. I have mentored many individuals online very successfully. However, there was one individual who gave me literally no feedback during our sessions. He muted his mike and if I asked a question, there was always a long period of time before he responded, and it was usually with a question for me to repeat my question. After a couple of days, I cut it off. I explained to him that we were wasting our time and while he may have the money to waste, I did not have the time to waste. I never heard from him again.

The important point I am trying to make is to continue to educate yourself. We live and work in a constantly changing world and investment environment. What worked a few years ago, does not work today. What works today, will not be relevant a few years from now. Also, there is always someone smarter than me who is developing some new technique, some not thought of interrelationship or some market anomaly. We should all want to know more of what is going on.

Therefore, set educational goals. Here is a list of what I suggest.

- Attend one seminar or convention before the end of the year.
- Read twelve books on economics, trading and investing by the end of the year
- Complete one course on trading and investing. It can be online,

from a book or you can attend a seminar.

- Join a trading group to meet people, either individually or in an online forum in order to share thoughts, ideas and experiences.

EQUIPMENT

When you setup your business, you may be able to buy the perfect computer system, install all of the perfect software, have the best desk and chair, and everything else to achieve success. However, if you are not that fortunate, then make a list of the tools you will need to continue to achieve the success you want.

When I first started in the business, I felt my way along slowly. I had one computer with one monitor. While the screen was not that big, the monitor took up most of the desk. Eventually, that monitor found its way to the junk yard and was replaced by two 15 inch flat screens. They progressed into larger screens and four monitors. Software was increased. The computers became faster. With each upgrade, I planned it. I knew what I had to do to get the equipment in terms of profits. When I achieved the internally generated profit, I invested in the equipment to improve the business.

Make a list of equipment you would like to have by the end of the first year. Set a goal for getting that equipment. Remember, your workplace is part of your vision. You may not have it setup exactly as your vision sees it, but you certainly have the ability to work toward that goal.

CHAPTER 7

STRENGTHS AND WEAKNESSES

ASSESSING YOUR STRENGTHS AND weaknesses is going to be critical to success in the investment world. Let me start with the most prevalent. Unless you are truly a different, you will have to deal with this particular weakness. If you don't, it will lead to the failure of your business. That weakness will pursue you throughout your career in the investment world. It will seduce you, nurture your thinking, make you complacent, and offer you any excuse you want for lack of performance. It will eventually take your capital and will leave you laying on the ground wondering what happened to your life. That weakness is pride. Pride is the heartbeat of resistance.

WEAKNESSES

When I wrote my first business plan for my trading business, I knew I had to go through an analysis of what were my strengths and weaknesses. I remember writing my strengths down. It seemed I had no problem listing them. Then, I started on weaknesses. After all, in any endeavor you want to maximize your strengths and minimize your weaknesses. Unfortunately, I struggled with the weaknesses. I simply didn't have any. The problem centered on my excitement over developing trading and investing as a business. I was overwhelmed with optimism. That led to ignoring my weaknesses because my strengths were running wild in my mind. I was sure of tremendous success.

To help, I decided to ask a couple of friends to write down on paper what they thought were my strengths and weaknesses. They responded to me very honestly. It was very humbling. A lot of the strengths I had outlined were there but not to the degree I saw myself. The weaknesses were like a lightning bolt. What surprised me most was two people had written my optimism as a weakness. After thinking about that for a while, I realized being too optimistic can be a weakness.

As I thought more about the weaknesses, I realized the greatest weakness I had was pride. While some optimism is good, too much will lead to pride. Additionally, in working with clients from around the world, I find the greater number of people have the same weakness when they enter this business, and it seems to infect the male investor more than the female investor. For the most part, women are more humble than men. Men, on the other hand have too much optimism and that leads to pride. We seem to have a "macho" attitude that we can do anything and we want to portray strength and success. Instead, we should cast off the "macho" and admit our weaknesses. Most of all, we should admit our failures. Not learning from failure, is a terrible weakness. It is pride that keeps us from learning and leads to destruction of capital.

I have to laugh sometimes when I work with a client and he starts out with a very manly attitude by almost beating his chest in his prowess to overcome and subdue the financial markets. This is usually where I begin. I start with trying to cut the roots of pride by questions directed toward their actual success as opposed to what they think in their minds. This usually stops the beating of the chest and we normally can get back to reality.

The worst case of pride to overcome is the new trader who has outstanding initial success. That success leads to pride and the feeling that they have arrived. They are now a professional trader. I have seen it many times. Once that occurs, it is just a matter of time before they blow up their account.

If there is one stumbling block that will lead to failure in this business it is pride. I have seen and experienced it in myself and in others. If you can overcome this one weakness, it will put you a long way down the path to success.

Proverbs 16:18 says, "Pride goes before destruction and a haughty spirit before a fall". No truer words were ever spoken for a trader.

The beginner in the trading and investing world will look at a chart of a financial instrument and will see a price trend. It looks so easy to buy the bottom and sell the high or sell the high and buy the bottom. They think they don't need anything else other than a chart and a trading platform. Pride tells them they can be an expert in no time. It is an easy business to enter and be successful. You don't need to educate yourself. There is no need to gain some experience. You are the next financial guru and television stations will be knocking down your door to interview you. Pride shows you your future bank account filled to the coffers. But, pride lies.

I remember when I first started in the business. I was trading Japanese Yen futures. I put the trade on when the currency futures market opened. It was a short trade. I sat there for a while waiting for the Yen to fall. It hesitated. I waited longer and it move up slightly. I was convinced it was headed lower so I held on. I told myself to be patient. Patience paid off. The Yen began to fall, but not just fall, it started to collapse right on my screen. I could see the profits building. I was up thousands of dollars in a matter of seconds.

Pride told me I had made it. I hit a home run. I was a financial genius. Instead of managing the trade, I got up from my desk, went to my wife and bragged to her how much money I had just made and all the things we were going to be able to do. She was very impressed with the new professional in the house. As I strolled back to my office thinking about how great it was to be a trader, I glanced at the screen. My stomach seemed to have a mind of its own because it was trying to come out of my mouth. I could not believe what I was seeing.

From the time I walked out of the office being up several thousand dollars, the Yen had rallied just as fast as it fell. In fact, it was above my entry point and I was down several hundred dollars. I hit the buy button as quickly as my shaking hands would move and exited the trade. Pride led me to brag about my position instead of managing my position.

I fell into my chair trying to keep my head from going through the monitor. Pride made me feel great. It had lifted me up. It told me I was a genius. I had made it. I was now a professional trader. I could support my family and have all the riches in the world. It had me feeling so good about myself, I didn't need to worry about a stop. I didn't have to care about trade or risk management. Pride had me leave the trade to the gremlins of the market. Pride had me boast of my prowess, while it was in the process of taking profits away and leaving me with nothing.

I have been in this business for over 30 years. That incident actually happened in my first year of trading and I remember it as if it happened yesterday. Pride still comes back to visit me periodically and we fight a lot, but most of the time I can prevail because pride's lessons are very painful.

I see pride in many individuals I work with. When they come to me for mentoring or consulting, I always ask how their performance is. The response is always they are doing great but just need a little help in this area or that. While that may be true for a few, it is not for the majority. Most come to me because they want to succeed in the business but they are not. Yet, they cannot admit it. They want me to believe they are successful. Pride tells them not to be honest with themselves and me. Pride keeps them from getting what they need.

The most successful individual I have ever worked with was able to get rid of pride very quickly. He came to me as a mentoring client. I live in North Carolina and he lives in California. We talked several times and he decided to work with me and I with him. I knew he was different when he told me he wanted to come spend a week with me. Before agreeing, I asked him what his performance was. This is when I knew I had a great client. He said he had put $150,000 in a trading account and had lost almost all of it. He explained that he had stopped trading until he could figure out what was wrong. He asked me to help him.

He came to my office and we worked for a solid week. Pride was not within him. There was one time we had done the analysis for a trade and he asked if he could actually take the trade, if the tactical entry appeared. I told him it would be fine and he opened his trading platform. The tactical entry appeared and he jumped in. Once in, he looked at me and asked where his stop should be. I smiled back and him and told him I didn't know. His eyes widened and I could see panic. This was the first trade he had made in months. The smile faded from his lips as he turned back to the market.

He turned to me again and asked where I suggest he put his stop. I guess he figured another way of asking the same question would help. I gave him the same answer. "I don't know." Then, I said, "Where do you think you should put the stop?" He looked at the chart and placed the stop. With that he managed the trade perfectly and exited with a nice profit.

When the trade was over, he had a smile on his face and thanked me. He had done it. More importantly, he sat staring at the screen going back over the trade, asking questions, suggesting alternative strategies and then planning for the next trade. Pride did not get in his way. He never let pride take over. Most importantly, he used a winning experience to improve on the next trade. He also knew to do that with the losing trades.

This individual eventually went on to make a great living for himself as a trader. The last time I spoke with him he was trading for other people and had developed a very successful business managing millions of dollars. Still, he gave all of the credit to his success to hard work of getting up many hours before the market opened, studying, planning and looking at all of the alternatives the market would give him that day and how he would react to each possible alternative. At the end of each day, he would review in detail his performance.

OTHER WEAKNESSES

EXPERIENCE

The ease of entry into the investment world is simple. Most people have a computer. All you need after that is a minimum of $2,500 to open a brokerage account and access to a system to begin an analysis procedure. I believe this is why the industry suggests that over 92% of people who enter the business fail. The lure is intoxicating. The ease of entry is tempting. The ability to be the master of your own destiny by sailing the financial waves draws many. Most of all, the simplicity of seeing a trend that developed in the past and thinking it is easy to buy the bottom and sell the top draws many into the slippery slope to losses.

You will need to assess your own experience. If you have none, admit it. If you have a little, acknowledge it. If there is much experience under your belt, it should be listed as a strength. However, whatever your level of experience, you will need to bring all of it to the table and then gain much more as you progress. I have never stopped learning. I always look for new ideas, and how to adapt to the changing economic environment.

Many times clients will expect me to offer some magic formula that will allow them to return home and immediately begin piling up profits. The magic formula comes from many hours of hard work, studying, analyzing, planning and executing. And, when the trade doesn't work and a loss is taken, using that experience to gain more knowledge for the next time.

If you are new in the investment world or don't feel you have much experience, then part of your plan should be to gain that experience. Outline the plan. Allow yourself to develop. You must pay for the education, no matter your level of experience. Therefore, keep the cost of the education as low as possible.

The first place to begin is to set a goal of self-education. That can come from a variety of methods: books, magazine articles, internet searches, courses, etc. Self-education will help you design a methodology. The methodology will then tell you when the market has setup for a possible trade. Remember, you are preparing a business plan. That must include education and training of the employees, meaning you!

Keep the cost of experience low. You don't have to start out trading futures. You don't have to begin by trading 1000 share lots. What is important is to produce results; to gain knowledge and experience. Remember, once you are consistent with a small lot, it is easy to add a zero to the lot size.

I should mention paper trading. I know a lot of people suggest paper trading to gain experience. That may be a good idea initially, especially if you are a true novice. However, I have always found there is a psychological disadvantage to paper trading. When you click the mouse and enter a paper trade, you know there is no risk. While you may want the trade to be profitable, you still have no "skin in the game". Therefore, I suggest moving to real-time trading as soon as possible, but do it with minimum risk. There is nothing wrong with trading 10 shares of a stock, or one option contract, especially with no or very low commissions. If you are insistent on trading futures, trade the future with the lowest cost. The S&P futures are $50 per point. NASDAQ futures are $20 per point. Reduce your educational and experience cost as much as possible. As you gain experience, then increase your trade size. Most all successful businesses begin small. As they gain knowledge and experience, they build on it to expand the business.

CAPITAL

The size of your capital account can be both a strength and a weakness. I have seen someone blow through a large brokerage account because they had too much money and it didn't mean much to them. On the other hand, I have worked with someone who could barely manage to put $10,000 into an account.

If you are truly drawn to the investment world and you believe the vision for your life can be enhanced through trading, then you must address capital. You cannot make a living with a $10,000 account. Therefore, you will have to find another way to pay your living expenses while you are developing the business. During that time, you will be able to gain tremendous knowledge and experience and may be able to grow your capital account to the point of being able to work full time.

Later I will discuss capital planning, but certainly your capital account needs to be considered as a strength or a weakness and then it has to be addressed as such. There is nothing wrong with starting with a $5,000 account. What is wrong is expecting to make $60,000 per year from that account.

TOOLS

You must have the proper tools to perform your role as a trader and investor. While you don't have to have the fastest and most elaborate, you do need to have sufficient tools in which to insure success. This means a computer system that will handle the programs you decide to use, the trading platform, and any other peripherals necessary for success.

When I first started in this profession, I had what I needed, not what I wanted. As success came, I started adding what I wanted. You can cut costs, but if you cut to the point of not being able to do your work, you are only sabotaging your own success.

You have to decide what you need and what you want. Fill the needs first. If you still have the means, then list your wants in order and fill those as you can.

ENVIRONMENT

The environment in which you choose to work is important. If there are a lot of distractions, it will affect your work. When you are deep into the analysis of an instrument and developing a plan for the next day, an interruption can send all of that work off to the distant past. If you are a day trader, is your office in a place where you can watch the markets throughout the day without interruption? Many times a trade tactic will appear and if not taken will disappear just as quickly.

Make sure that others in your home or wherever you are understand the importance of not being disturbed during the time you are working. It is certainly okay to take time off for lunch, or even take the day off early, but that needs to be your decision on when to do it and when not to.

In addition to the above, the economic environment changes all of the time. Fluctuations in the financial environment will change the perception of value on the part of other traders and investors. Know when a potential change is coming. Set alerts for when important news releases are being made. Also, keep an eye on geopolitical events. The economic world is very intertwined. A negative news event outside of the US can have a major impact on financial markets.

RESOURCES

Do you have the proper resources? One to consider is a support group. For me, my clients are my support group. I have learned a tremendous amount from teaching and educating them. In fact, some of the best ideas I use now have come from discussions with clients. There are lots of trader groups around that you can join. If there is not one in your area, find one online. It may be a chat group, or something more elaborate, but join one. I was once invited to one on Facebook and found many of the posts very informative. However, stay away from chat groups where you are following the trades of the moderator. That is simply being a trading robot. Do your own work. Gain your own experience. Avoid a trading room where you follow the trade of the moderator.

Your broker is probably the most important resource. If you are trading equities and paying up to $1.00 - $9.00 per trade, you are paying too much. Those are supposedly the discount brokers, but there are brokers out there who are charging $1.00 per trade turn and most recently nothing. As I write this, the largest online brokers have announced no commissions. This, in itself, can add much to your financial performance. Also, does your broker provide charts? Many do for just opening the account. The only thing you have to pay are the exchange fees and a lot of times you are paying them anyway.

STRENGTHS

Your strengths will be easy to identify, as mine were. Remember, we want to identify strengths and weaknesses in an effort to capitalize on our strengths and minimize weaknesses or overcome them. Since I began the weaknesses section with pride, I must begin the strength section with humility. It is probably the most important strength you can have. If you don't have it, then you need to develop it. The financial markets have a way of making the most prideful very humble.

HUMILITY

The opposite of pride is humility. If you are humble, you need to put that at the top of the list. If you can admit your failures, your mistakes and the fact that you are not yet the next Jesse Livermore, then you have tremendous strength.

I write a newsletter for traders and investors. In those newsletters I talk about successful trades and losing trades. I received an email from a client one day and he explained how helpful the newsletter was to him. He said that not only does he learn from my good trades but the losing ones as well. He went on to say it also helped him to realize that not all trades are successful and that in itself gave him more confidence. It takes strength to face a loss, admit it and then take it. Strength comes from analyzing and learning from that loss.

I will say this. If you don't have humility, the gremlins of the market have it as their one objective to give you humility. They seduce you with pride and when your head is laying on your desk and you are wondering what happened to your capital account, you can hear them laughing. That is the time when you can accept and admit you need humility. Humility will keep the market gremlins away. Humility relates back to ROC and position sizing. A humble trader will have a reasonable ROC and manage risk through position sizing.

Everything that pride is, humility is not. Humility allows you to admit you are inexperienced. It drives you to seek advice, to study, to self-educate. More importantly, humility will bring you to admit what you are doing is not working. It will force you to stop, reassess, try again and continue the process until you have achieved success. I have spoken at many seminars and conventions. I always mingle with the other people there and join in conversations. I want to learn from them. I want to hear their thoughts, ideas and strategies. I will talk about my losses as much as my gains.

There is no other profession in which you can sit down at a computer, open an brokerage account and compete with people all over the world. The cost of entering is cheap and alluring. The end cost can be dramatic. That is why humility will have us check ourselves constantly. Pride has us march on into the hail of market ticks, as if our accounts are limitless.

Humility will let you listen to someone with more experience and not feel as if you have to prove your prowess. This strength will give you sweet lessons in experience without having to pay for them. You can listen, observe and allow others' glories and failures to become your own. All of this must be filtered carefully so we know who is speaking from pride and who from humility.

I have said it before and I will say it again. There is no "holy grail" in the trading and investment world. If there is, it is the ability to put everything discussed in this book together and then execute. Therefore, you must educate yourself in various methodologies. Developing trade strategies and tactics will take time. Testing them will take more time and money. But, with each attempt you will learn more and gain more experience.

Years ago, I was a firm believer in Elliott Wave Theory. I was stellar at counting market waves in various time-frames. It worked perfectly. Then, it didn't. I kept with it but the losses kept mounting. I could not figure it out. A few months went by and I knew I had to stop trading. Elliott Wave was simply not working. The market had moved on and was developing outside of Mr. Elliott's theory. When I stopped and studied the market, I could see how the theory was simply not working, at least at that time. I needed a new methodology.

I spent time studying other analysis techniques. All of the time the revenues were stagnant. No trades were made. Weeks turned into a month, then two. Then one day, I was looking at the charts and I saw it. I was able to see the exact method of how to build a strategy for each day and the tactical entries jumped out of the screen at me. For the next two weeks, I continued watching and studying. I still did not trade.

I didn't realize it at the time but I had become a student of the markets. Then one day, I saw the strategy develop and the tactical entry jumped out at me again. I took the trade and it was very profitable. I was back! I still see Elliot waves in charts and at times that experience is very helpful, but I now have a much better methodology that has proved its success over and over.

The important part of that story is the fact I took the time to study and develop a new methodology. I didn't force the trades. My capital account did not grow but it did not decrease either. We must always be open to learning from ourselves, others and experience. The markets are made up of humans. People have emotions. Therefore, the collective grouping of market participants creates a behavioral pattern. That behavior will change over time as the economic environment changes. We, as traders, must also change when necessary.

EXPERIENCE

There is a saying, "A man with experience met a man with money. Shortly thereafter, the man with the experience had the money and the man with the money had the experience". This is the case of the markets. It is why I stress with clients who do not have great experience to begin slowly with small amounts. You must gain experience and to do that you want to keep the cost of that experience as low as possible.

When I stopped using Elliot Wave Theory, I didn't throw it completely away. Deep inside me, I have knowledge and experience from the days of using it that are still valuable. Many times in multiple time-frames you can see a countertrend rotation develop in three steps. I still teach that to clients and how to identify whether a move is impulsive or if it is countertrend and the main impulsive move may be about to exert itself once again. That is important information to have.

Many times someone will enter a trade after identifying a trend, only to have it reverse against them immediately. What they did not see was in the next greater degree timeframe it was a countertrend move and the main trend had just re-exerted itself. Draw from all of your experiences in the markets. You may not use them but sometime off in the distance you will see something, an experience will trigger a memory and you will jump on it.

Important to experience is learning from our failures. It frustrates me to no end when failures are ignored. If I review a losing trade with a client and they shrug it off with some excuse, I usually get very stern. That losing trade is an education they paid for. It is an experience that cost them money. Why would they just let it go with some lame excuse?

I encourage clients to make notes on all of their trades, both winning and losing. However, it is the losing trades that will provide you with the greatest amount of wealth in terms of experience. Never let a losing trade go into the trash without studying it until you found all of the things you misread from the market; the tactics that were in error; the trade management that was non existent; or the pride that had you greedy to be in a trade that was a high risk low reward situation.

Summary

In any business you have to understand what your strengths and weaknesses are. In our business weaknesses are prevalent. Therefore, it is critical to success to define our weaknesses. We must recognize and admit to them. Once we do that, we have chosen a path to eliminating them and potentially making them a strength. Ignoring losses will only make that weakness greater.

Each individual will have their own strengths and weaknesses. I have found engineers to be stronger in their ability to analyze. Computer programmers are excellent in analysis. Each of these individuals have an issue with risk. Sometimes they look to minimize risk too much when they should trust the analysis and let the profits run. Others skip the analysis, jump in the market only to get run over in a trade. They eventually will cut their profits short and allow their losses to run, thinking the market will come back.

List your strengths and weaknesses. If you have trouble, as I did, enlist the help of spouse, friend, or anyone who knows you well enough to give you honest answers. Be humble about the answers you receive.

CHAPTER 8

ENVIRONMENTAL ASSESSMENT

The Physical Environment

HE ENVIRONMENTAL ASSESSMENT SHOULD take two forms. The first is the environment you will have created in which to work. This is extremely important and should take thought and planning.

You will need to have the proper tools and the right place in which to run your business. Even if you are doing it part time, the tools and environment are critical. If you don't have the proper tools, then you have set yourself up for excessive costs through trade losses. Remember, when planning your business, get what you need, not what you want. If you can afford the wants also, that is great. However, do not be cheap on the needs. A few extra hundred dollars or a thousand that will help you save thousands or make thousands is money well spent.

To decide on the environment you will operate in, you will first need to begin with some type of methodology. We will discuss more about methodology later, but you must have some idea of how you will analyze the markets, decide on how to approach each day, tactical entries, and how you will manage each trade. The methodology you decide on will give you your first look at the tools necessary.

I spoke at a regional meeting of traders, using charts from a chart vendor in which I prepare a strategy each day. There happened to be a distributor of charts at the meeting promoting their system. After my presentation, one of them approached me and wanted to show me a similar chart their program could produce. I looked at it but it was definitely inferior. The difference was, if I opened a brokerage account with them the charts were free. I could probably save an extra hundred or two hundred dollars a month, but the cost of using an inferior program was likely higher.

When you enter the big leagues of trading and investing, you don't want to compete with inferior tools. After all, if you can't make the extra hundred dollars trading your methodology, then something is wrong and you need to stop trading and reassess what you are doing.

If your computer will not run your chart program, broker platform and any other tools you need, then you need a new computer. If your charts are not giving you the information you really need to do a thorough analysis, then you need a new chart program. If the chair you sit in all day gives you back pain, then you need a new chair. Do you need eight computer monitors? Probably not. Do you want eight monitors? You decide.

Decide what you need to be successful. When the success comes, treat yourself to some of your wants, especially if they will enhance your work environment. A positive work environment has been shown to produce positive results, no matter the business field you are in.

I want to address one more item in the physical environment. That is the area in which you work. Whether it be on a full or part time basis, that area is an inner sanctum that needs to be revered. When I first started trading, I had an office in a separate bedroom. It was very small and cramped but when I went into the office, the kids knew that Dad was at work.

Where you work is a place in which you enter the maze of financial analysis. It is where you look for the clues the market is sending. You decide what is important and what is not. You interpret the small nuances of the behavior of the instrument of your choice. From there, your work takes a form. As it develops, you begin to see a picture of what the market is attempting to say to you and others. Piercing the veil of hidden meanings, your strategy begins to develop and finally you end with a probability of one event occurring over another and you know exactly what you will do in the coming day.

Trying to do all of that work and being interrupted, or not having an environment in which you enjoy working will affect the quality of work you do. The quality of work will have a direct impact on your performance. Poor quality is unacceptable to the shareholder who owns the capital account.

One of my clients was a young executive who decided to become a full time trader. He had made a lot of money and had the ability to leave his position and start his own trading business. He setup an office in a separate room. His two young children knew when he was in the office with the door closed they were not supposed to interrupt him unless it was an emergency. His wife agreed to the same.

The problem was he prepared his analysis in the morning. That was the time when the kids were getting ready to go to school and his wife was heading out to work. The environment was still not working. It was causing chaos with the kids and unnecessary pressure with his wife who had to get the kids and herself ready and out the door. A change was needed.

He decided he would get up two hours earlier. He had the morning completely to himself in quiet, while the rest of the family slept. When they rose, he was finished with the analysis and was able to be with his children and wife before they left for the day and he returned to his office to start the trading session. He eventually became one of my most successful clients.

Sometimes we have to be flexible, especially if we have families and are working from home. That means being flexible with the environment, the hours the environment is sacred and the priorities we have in our life. Of course, if you are single, the only environment you will need to manage is when the dog gets taken out for a walk.

The environment in which we choose to work is important. We are searchers and investigators. We we look for the subtle pieces of information that hide in the jumble of world financial markets. We seek to pry out those prized nuggets that give us just a small hint of where the markets will be marching in the coming day. To do that we need the proper environment, and once we delve into the caverns of price moves, we need not be drawn back out until those prized pieces of information have been extracted, analyzed and properly put into a place that will bring us the sweet victory of another successful trade.

MARKET ENVIRONMENT

Just as important as the physical environment, is the market environment. The markets are not static. They are not some machine that chugs through the day churning out price movements randomly and our job being to judge the direction of that randomness. The markets are made up of human beings. Those individuals have thoughts, desires, concepts, and most of all emotions. What each of them have is the desire to search for value in the financial markets. The search for value causes some to seek value higher, while others anticipate value is too high and price will revert back to some former level. It is that interaction that gives us price discovery. One day those who seek higher value will win. The next it may be the opposite. Therefore, our job is to try to determine where value will be found. It is called Price Discovery. To do that, we will need to extract information from the participants as to who will be stronger and which will be weaker. Then, we invest our hard earned money with the stronger. Basically, we are looking for trends in the time-frame we choose to trade. But, those trends can change in an instant.

If there is one important nugget you get from this book, it should be: the markets are a collective gathering of people who at times will make no sense and at others will appear perfectly logical. Once we have a high probability of the direction of the market, it is also important to understand the strength or weakness of the directional move. Investing in a trend that is weakening, as it comes into support or resistance, can produce significant losses.

I like to look at a the markets as a life form. It takes a shape. It lives. It breathes. It expresses the emotions of the collective crowd. We are lured into it thinking we understand it. Just when we do, it morphs into something completely different. It changes shape. It begins acting like something we have never seen before. The mistake many make is to not change with the market.

Earlier I wrote about my studies of Elliott Wave Theory. I was very successful using that methodology for a time. The markets cooperated perfectly. Looking for third waves got easier and easier with each passing day. Then, one day the waves stopped. No analysis I performed worked. The strategic and tactical rules I used only proved to strip me of profits I longed to receive. The market had morphed. Human behavior in financial instruments stopped moving impulsively in five waves and correcting in three.

Because the market changed its behavior, I had to adapt and change as well. After spending time studying and trying to figure out what was really going on, it was clear. The market behavior had moved on and left me sitting looking at the waves. It was time to morph into a new methodology. Certainly, I drew from all of the other experiences I had up to that point. Chart patterns, moving averages, stochastics, and any other technical method was brought out of the closet.

I had to figure out how to develop a new methodology. Figuring out how to analyze the markets and the tools to use became critical. It was time to stop trading. Once I figured it out, I tested it by watching and studying price movement. Then, as discussed above,

I stuck my toes in the water and then waded in deeper and deeper as I became more confident.

I think two examples are important here. I meet a lot of investors who establish a set of rules for trading. Rules are good, but rules also need to be adapted as the environment changes. Most will remember the Long Term Capital Management fiasco from the nineties. They developed a computer model that took advantage of the spread between sovereign debt and interest rates. The computer had identified the human behavior of what occurs when various anomalies exist in sovereign debt markets. They made billions. It was tremendously successful. It was so successful they were able to leverage the firm by billions. The problem was the behavior of the sovereign debt market changed. The computer was not programed to anticipate the change of human behavior. The result from a lack of understanding the changing environment almost froze the entire financial system.

The second is being aware of events that occur periodically that will have the potential to change the perception of value by participants in a market or a specific instrument. An example is a Federal Reserve meeting and the announcement of interest rates, employment numbers, earnings releases, etc. All of these can have the potential of changing the directional movement of price. It is important to be aware of these events, allow the crowd to sort through value discovery and when that is complete, we can then find good tactical entries.

In the same regard as above, the trader who establishes a set of technical rules to follow without understanding the environment of the market he or she is trading may find initial success, but in the end, as the markets morph, they will find some things simply will not work in a changing financial environment. As an example, there are many times a trader using a stochastic indicator, buying the crosses up and selling the crosses down, will do well. However, what happens on the day the indicator is overbought and crosses down but price keeps going higher?

My point is: we must be familiar with the environment we are trading and investing in. Important to that understanding is knowing when information can come into the environment that will change it.

There are other such times also when value will differ from what it was in the past. I knew a trader once who felt he had to trade the markets based only on what he saw in the charts. He had a strict discipline and wanted no outside influence on his technical analysis. The problem was he would periodically get run over when there was some type of news event he was not aware of. He was a good analyst and he was mostly profitable. However, there were times when he could have avoided losses by simply being aware of the potential for a changing environment.

Another great example is inter-market relationships. We have all seen one market trade with or against another market. Those relationships exist for a time and then they decouple. That is a result of a change in the environment of those instruments and the perception of value that has changed due to the behavior of the traders who are involved in those markets.

Dow Theory, in summary, says a bull market will continue as long as the Dow Industrials are confirmed by the Dow Transports. In other words, they should trade together. However, there are times when they diverge. This theory suggests that when they do diverge, it is a warning of an impending trend change. As I write this, the Industrials are making new all-time highs, but the Transports are not. That suggests the anticipation on the part of buyers of Industrial stocks may be overvalued because the companies that transport the goods sold by the Industrials are slowing down. It is an environmental warning of a possible trend change.

Finally, we always want to invest with the "herd" or the larger money. Once again, we do not want to ignore warning signs of the herd potentially running over a cliff. When we see those signs, it is time to begin stepping aside. A great example was the tech bubble in the year 2000. Everyone was making money in stocks. Start-ups with no earnings were being bid up hundreds of dollars per share in anticipation of potential earnings. Understanding the environment, many were able to get out and book profits and others went short. It was obvious the herd was heading for the cliff at top speed.

Always try to understand the current environment of the market you are trading and when that environment may change.

CHAPTER 9

ORGANIZING FOR SUCCESS

I F YOU WERE PLANNING to open a business, you would complete a lot of research into the market you are entering; the cost of entering that business; how your product or service is going to be produced; and analyzed your competition. Many business plans for successful entrepreneurs are written in different forms. Some are written on a few sheets of paper, while even more are well thought out and documented.

There is no one form for success. The important part is that some form of planning be accomplished. Not only will it give you the path to the vision you have created but it will help you in determining whether you are on that path or not. Important to the success of the plan is how you organize your venture. That is also true in the business of trading and investing.

Most start out in the business by simply sitting down at our computers, pulling up some sort of technical software and trading with a broker on their online platform. That works initially. However, there are other very important aspects to consider.

LEGAL

Some will incorporate a Subchapter S corporation, a Limited Partnership, if others may be involved, or a Limited Liability Company. This book is not intended to give legal advice. Therefore, before doing any form of incorporation, I suggest discussing it with an adviser or an attorney. For one thing, the cost of formation is typically a few hundred dollars and the cost to maintain it in the state you reside can be significant. Additionally, you will have a separate tax return to prepare that will add to the cost as well.

I started out by simply opening everything in my personal name and included profits and losses on my personal tax return. Later, as the business developed, I formed a Limited Partnership and then a Limited Liability Company. But, in my case, I was forming a fund and wanted to bring in other investors. Therefore, you may not need to incorporate. This is why it is important to know the vision you have for the business and seek the proper advice.

TAX

Once again, it is not my intention to give tax or accounting advice, but there are some significant impacts on how you organize. As an example, when I filed as an individual, my short term gains were only offset by short term losses. Longer term positions had the benefit of being taxed at long term capital gains rates. When I started, there were initial losses, those losses could only be deducted to the maximum of $3,000 per year. However, they did accumulate and later were offset against the profits.

You will also have the choice of choosing to be taxed as a professional trader or not. This allows you to take advantage of certain write off of expenses you would not normally be able to do. Whether you choose to do this or not, should be given careful thought and discussed with your tax adviser.

EDUCATION

Every business that starts up has a cost of starting the business. While most of us already have many of the tools we need to get into trading and investing, you will need to plan on an educational cost. That cost is directly related to books, and other educational material, and more importantly to experience. If you are fairly new to this industry and you think you will not have a cost for experience, you need to go back and read the chapter on Strengths and Weaknesses again. There is always a cost.

MARKETS

It is important to choose the markets you trade carefully. I have never understood why some individuals insist on trading the futures market with little or no experience. There are so many other alternatives that will not be as volatile, costly and can give you the experience you need before stepping into that fierce arena.

My personal experience was to begin with stocks. I later used a basic option strategy and then began looking at the futures market. If you are into sitting in front of your computer and day trading, then futures may be for you. However, if you are more interested in analyzing different instruments, evaluating reward and risk, spreading risk and having the ability to get up from the computer to go have lunch, then you should consider another market than the futures. Trading in equities and options will also give you the opportunity to trade in multiple timeframes.

I encourage my beginners to start with a stock index ETF. There are many that track the various Indices. There are even double and triple leveraged ETFs. These ETFs move double or triple the move of the underlying Index. If your knowledge and experience are limited, why trade a S&P futures contract that can cost you $50 per point, when you can gain the same knowledge and experience trading 10 shares of the S&P ETF: SPY at $10 per point? If you can trade ten shares profitably, then you can trade 100. If you can trade 100 profitably, then you can trade 1000. At that point, if you want to dip your feet into the futures arena, then you probably have what it takes in terms of knowledge and experience.

In the US markets there are probably close to 10,000 stocks that trade with enough volume to be considered. One of the most important things to remember is if your analysis works in one instrument, it will most likely work in all instruments. I have seen one client after another insist on trading one futures market and that is all. When that market goes into a rotational pattern, they feel they have to trade every day. Forcing a trade in a market that is in short term rotation will cause you to get chopped up. Why not set an alert to let you know when a breakout occurs and then begin looking to other instruments to find one that will provide what you are looking for? Personally, I prefer to watch various instruments and then take a position in the one offering the greater reward to risk. Someone else may look to only one or two instruments and focus on those only. In that case, they will have to have patience in order not to force trades.

BROKERS

Once you have decided on the instruments you are going to trade, you will then have to decide on a broker. Some brokers are only futures brokers. Others are only stock brokers. Still others are a combination of both. Your choice of a broker should be important and they should be able to fill the needs of your business. Remember, you are their customer. If they cannot give you what you are looking for, look for another.

Commission rates are critical. It is a cost of doing business. Consider a futures trader who pays $8.00 per round turn. If he is a day trader in the S&P futures, each point he makes will net him only $42.00, whereas, the trader who pays a commission of half that will take home $46.00 per point. That may not seem like much but when you are an active trader, it mounts up. Now, there are many equity brokers who do not charge commissions. This is a tremendous advantage if you are new to investing and want to trade smaller lot sizes or if you are trying out different tactical entries.

Finally, all brokers provide charts. The quality and accuracy of the chart will be very important. The last thing you need is a broker's charts that keep crashing periodically or are only refreshing every few seconds. The charts should refresh with every tick. I had several clients complain about one broker's trade platform and charts that kept freezing up on them. Several different people complained about it. My advice was that it was unacceptable and they should immediately move on to another broker. Recently, I heard that broker had solved its charting and platform issues.

Also, investigate the cost of any charting program. Most brokers will pass on to you the Exchange Fees. They vary in the markets you decide to trade. However, some also will tack on a premium to that fee. Investigate the cost. I have seen some very astute individuals, who supposedly know what they are doing, using a broker platform that is charging them excessive fees.

I have used for many years and I am still using Investor/RT charts. They are excellent. The analysis tools they offer with the program are far superior to others I have looked at (www.linnsoft.com)

Chart Programs

You will have to decide on a charting program, if you haven't already. Your charting program must give you the tools you need to perform your profession. This is an area where you need to be smart but don't deny yourself the tools you need to be successful. I spend a little more on my charting program because it is necessary to me in my analysis. There are other cheaper programs and one more expensive for my analysis technique, but I have a good relationship with the company that produces them and they give me everything I need and want from an analysis perspective.

Because I use the Market Profile(tm) charts extensively, I love the Investor/RT platform (www.linnsoft.com).

I recently found a service that offers free charts. I have been trying it out and it appears excellent. There is a premium version for less than $20 per month and exchange fees are very reasonable. Check out www.tradingview.com. Whatever it takes, keep the cost of your business when you start as low as possible, but don't put your success at risk by going too cheap. You have to keep an eye on costs but your ultimate goal is performance.

Most important is your charting program must support your trade methodology. If it does not, then you will obviously not be able to develop a good strategy.

Record Keeping

There will be much more on this in the chapter on Controlling the Trader, but how you keep your records will be very important. You need to organize in the beginning to track your success and failure. I have seen many, (I was guilty of it myself when I first started.), who neglect record keeping. Think about it this way. If you gave your money to someone to trade for you, wouldn't you want to know almost daily how he was doing? I would. Therefore, you would ask him to keep certain records. You may not call every day but you would want to know how he is doing when you do call and would like to have at least a monthly analysis of his/her performance.

I keep a spreadsheet and log each day's activity. That is totaled by month and then there is a link to the performance for the year. As each day is entered, it updates the monthly progress and that updates the yearly progress. Seeing my performance keeps me honest and honesty with ourselves is critical to our success. Everyone goes through a slump. It is easy to shrug off losses and not want to look at them. However, at some point you will need to face them, especially if they keep mounting. There must come a time, when that happens, the shareholder takes the trader out to the woodshed for a good talking to. In reality, you must know when to stop trading. When you do stop, it will provide you with the most important information on what you may be doing wrong, a possible change in the environment of the markets you trade, or something completely unrelated to the markets themselves.

HARDWARE

I have discussed previously the difference between needs and wants in terms of hardware, office space, etc. As a business you want to keep your expenses as low as possible, but you don't want to keep them so low you are not able to perform your job because you don't have the proper tools. Therefore, the decision process you go through will be very important.

If you can get by with two monitors to begin, that is great. I worked with someone who had eight monitors. That was too many for me. I found myself not working but just looking from one monitor to the next to see what was happening. Personally, I used four monitors for a long time, but have recently retired one of those and am now using three very efficiently.

I had a very successful client who only used two monitors. He used to say that monitors are like martinis. One is not enough and three are too many. I'm not sure about three because that is what I use but I am sure about one. It is simply not enough. You will need one monitor to watch the market you are trading and another for your trade platform to execute tactically and for trade management.

OFFICE

Your choice of office will depend on whether you are a part time investor or a day trader. It will also depend on your home and family. If there is a room in which you can not be disturbed and perform your analysis, then that will work. If you are part time, you may use a common room with a computer in it, but you will need to be able to concentrate. Ninety-nine percent of the work you do will be in the analysis function. 1% of the time you will be entering and exiting trades. Trade management is extremely important and that falls under the analysis time. Once the trade moves in the direction you want, you will need to manage it properly.

Finally, think through all of the aspects of setting up and running a trade and investment business. If you are beginning or are doing it part time, you don't need to jump in over your head. Take your time. Investigate and evaluate, then make well informed decisions.

CHAPTER 10

DEVELOPING STRATEGIES

THE GREATEST WEAKNESS I have found in working with individuals in this business is they think it is an easy career. It is so simple to look at a chart and see a market trend, observe a technical indicator and see two lines cross and assume a trade can be made easily. This leads the individual to laziness. That in turn opens the door to entering trades without knowing where there is good trade location. Too often, I hear investors state they feel the market knows they are entering a position because it always reverses as soon as they enter. This is more often than not a case of poor trade location. It is a lack of understanding where areas of support and resistance are in various time-frames and the strength of the instrument going into those areas of support or resistance.

Before going much farther, let me first state the mistake most people bring to their trading is that of not having a strategy. They simply want to know when to enter and when to exit. Therefore, it is important to distinguish between strategy and tactics. If you simply look at a chart and project your feeling on where the instrument is going and trade on that alone, you are setting yourself up for failure. Success in the investment field takes work. All of the work is done before entering the trade. If you eliminate that, you will find your capital dwindling. Therefore, there are two important aspects of every trade: strategy and tactics. You must have a good strategy and you must know how to execute tactically on the strategy.

STRATEGY

A definition of strategy is found in Wikipedia. It states, "Strategy is a high level plan to achieve one or more goals under unknown conditions of uncertainty". Remember the business of trading and investing is mostly a series of probability assessments. You seek information from the market and then decide the higher probability of one event occurring over another. In most cases it is the higher probability of an instrument going up over it going down. However, if we limit the probability assessment to just one instance, then we may have eliminated a potential opportunity. This assumes you have the propensity to short a market. Even if you don't have that propensity, it may behoove you to exit a long trade or be aware of a potential decline of more than you are willing to accept in terms of losses.

In strategic development your goal is to determine if the market does this, then you will do that. If the market does that, then you will do this. There will be times when you come into the day thinking you have a sound strategy and the market throws you a curve and does something completely unexpected. When that occurs, the best strategy is to stand aside until the market gives you more information. Remember, trading is being long. Trading is being short. Trading is standing aside when you are unsure.

Your first step is to build a strategy for each day. In this case I am referring to whatever time-frame you trade or invest in. Even if you are a long term investor, you should review and monitor all positions on a daily basis. With each day, the market will give you information that is extremely important. It may suggest you hold your position, sell, or to move your stop. The old buy and hold strategy has long been dismissed as erroneous. Just think back to those who held long positions in 2000 and 2008. It took the first sixteen years to get back to where they were in 2000 and the later took eight years to get back to break even.

How you develop a strategy will take some time and some work. I want to stress once again. There is no solid strategy for winning in the market. The person who puts in the most work will gain the most reward. There are also many successful strategies that you can use or develop. It is not the purpose of this book to spend time giving you the strategy I use. That will be handled in the next book in great detail showing strategy development and tactical entries. However, I will give you an idea of the process I go through to find support and resistance in multiple time-frames and develop a strategy for each day.

Step 1 - Decide the time-frame you will trade or invest in. Then, begin analyzing the instrument in the next greater degree time-frame. If you will be using daily charts, then start analyzing the market with a weekly chart. Once you understand the trend and where important support and resistance areas are, drop down to a daily chart. Compare how the instrument is developing on a daily basis and then look for your entry points.

If you are a short term swing trader and use a thirty or sixty minute chart then you will want to know the degree of trend on an hourly, one hundred-twenty minute basis and possibly a daily basis. Day traders using a five or one minute chart will want to know the development of price on a thirty and sixty minute basis.

Understanding the development of price or the trend in the next greater degree of time will give you important information as to whether you are entering a trade in a counter-trend move or trading with the main trend. It will give you support and resistance areas. It is important to remember the greater the degree of time, the greater the money that controls that time-frame. You always want to invest with larger money. That is why it is so important to understand the development of price in a larger time-frame.

A day trader using a one or five minute chart may see a trend developing. However, if that person ignores what is happening in a thirty or sixty minute time-frame, they may find the trend they are looking at is the completion of a counter-trend move and the main trend is getting ready to re-exert itself. That is when the novice trader or investor typically gets "run over". If there is one thing you take away from this chapter, I hope it is to understand, at a minimum, the development of price in multiple time-frames.

Step 2 - Analyze and assess the environment of the instrument you are trading. It is important to remember the value of any instrument is solely determined by the collective will of the individuals who have chosen to trade and invest in that instrument. You will want to know if there is information that may be coming into the market that could change the determination of value on the part of those individuals. Never take for granted good information will be good for price or bad information will be bad for price. In most cases that will be the case. However, there are many times when a company will come out with earnings above forecast and the stock immediately sells off. Even recently in the Stock Indices themselves information that should be bad for Stocks has sent the Indices soaring because it suggested the Fed will not raise interest rates. Alternatively, good information for stocks has sent the markets lower for the exact opposite reason. Remember, you are trying to find the direction the majority of investors are going and you want to go with them.

You may not be able to predict the reaction of the participants to the information but you will be able to have a strategy that will give you a tactical move no matter what the result of that environmental change on the development of price. As an example, you have a position in XYZ stock and you are currently holding a profit. You know that analysts have predicted excellent revenues and earnings for the release that will occur tomorrow. What you do not know is whether XYZ will meet, fail or exceed those expectations. Therefore, you build a strategy that says if XYZ moves up to this point, you will exit and book the profit, move your stop up, add to your position, or do nothing. Alternatively, if it falls, you develop a corresponding strategy to allow your stop to be hit and book the profit, see if it holds at support and add to your position or do nothing.

In each case above, it is a strategy. Since we cannot predict successfully the reaction of participants to any environmentally changing information, we have developed a strategy for each possible event.

Tactics would tell you where the stock would go for you to exit, move your stop, etc.

Step 3 - Analyze the structure of the development of price in multiple time-frames. When we look at price development, we are looking at the trend of price. When we look at price structure, we are looking at the internals that make up the development of price and the structure of that particular trend.

In Step 1 above, we found where support and resistance in multiple time-frames. Step 2 gave us an understanding of whether there was information that could come into the market that might change the determination of value or literally make the trend change. Step 3 gives us an understanding of whether the instrument is strengthening or weakening going into that support or resistance. There are many technical indicators that will help you in determining strength or weakness. The prime indicator I use is a nine period exponential moving average of volume. If you don't have a program that can give you a moving average of volume, then just use raw volume in the time-frame you are investing in. Volume tells me, as an instrument is approaching support or resistance, the strength of the participants driving the move.

If I am investing with the trend, I want to know that others are supporting that trend. Volume gives me the indication of whether a stock is being acquired as it moves up or if buyers are waning. If volume is falling off, it is a clear indication the trend may be exhausting itself.

There is an old saying, "The trend is your friend". I would add to that, "The trend is your friend and volume tells you if it will stay your friend". In addition to volume there are other indicators that make up a combination of volume, price and other statistical information. I use the Relative Strength Index (RSI) periodically. Accumulation Distribution Index (AD) is also another one to consider. Finally, the Volume Weighted Average Price (VWAP) is excellent. Whatever you decide, do some research on the indicator you choose and be sure that as one of the calculations volume is included. Additionally, test out three or four to see which you prefer. There are many times I will add a new indicator that includes volume just to get another picture of what may be happening inside of the development of price.

Step 4 - In developing a strategy you have made a probability assessment of one event occurring over another. As an example, I have assessed the probabilities of XYZ stock continuing in its uptrend. Volume is supporting it and while it will approach longer term resistance, I feel the higher probability is for a continuation of the up move, after a possible pause at resistance. That is all based on the information the market has given me about XYZ up to the point I developed the strategy.

What is important now is to recognize the fact that I have just made a probability assessment and decided a greater probability of the trend continuing through resistance. What is extremely important for me to keep in mind now is there is also a lower probability I am wrong and the stock will exhaust itself going into resistance and begin some type of rotation down. Based on this, I must have a strategy should the lower probability occurrence become the greater probability. In this way, when the market opens and XYZ begins trading, I have a strategy for one event occurring over another. I am not blindsided.

It may be I have analyzed an instrument that I want to invest in. I know it is approaching resistance and expect a pause, as instruments typically do around support and resistance. Therefore, I know it is an area of good trade location. I then develop a strategy that says, if the stock goes through resistance and volume is increasing, I will buy. If the stock, after a pause at resistance, begins to trade lower outside of that pause, I will sell the stock short. This type of strategy is extremely important to the short term traders and investors.

Step 5 - There will be a time when you should stand aside. After spending time doing the analysis and developing a strategy for the coming day, the market may do something you do not expect. In this case, the information you received from the market was not sufficient, the determination of price value changed, or you were simply wrong in your planning. In this case, it is best to take a breath, exercise some patience and wait.

This is a good time to mention gaps. There are many times I have done the work of analyzing, developed a strategy, and was ready to enter the next day, only to find the instrument has opened with a gap in the direction of my analysis. In other words it came into resistance in the case of an uptrend and instead of trading through it, there was a gap that took the stock well above resistance.

In the above case, I have found that chasing a market can prove disastrous. When a gap happens I typically will stand aside. I put a notch in my belt for doing the analysis correctly. It is obvious there were a lot of other people who did the analysis and came to the same conclusion. Over night the buy orders at the open simply caused a gap. Many times, there will be a gap and then there is no follow through and price retraces back to resistance that is now support. There are many opportunities in the markets, if we miss one, there will be another. Try not to chase price.

There are some excellent tactical entries short-term traders can use on gap days. So, if the strategy is correct and the stock gaps, don't ignore the short-term possibilities that could turn into a swing trade or better.

TRADE LOCATION

I want to make one more point concerning trade location. After using many different techniques to develop trade strategy, I found a very useful tool in the Time Price Opportunity charts. These charts lean heavily on price over a given period of time and volume. It is easy to see where market participants have found value in the past and where they have found price to be unfair. It is at these unfair price levels the best trade location can be found. More importantly, there are times when an unfair price level will be the same in multiple timeframes. This offers a tremendous opportunity to the trader/investor.

Multiple timeframe trade location means it has the attention of short term money up to much longer term larger money. These are where the best moves are made. While they may not come often, when they do, the opportunity exists to add a very nice profit to your capital account.

If you are not familiar with them, Time Price Opportunity Charts (TPO) show the price level where each trade is made. Along with that, they display volume at price. This can be important information in strategic development. The chart shows where traders have found price to be unfair (support and resistance). Volume shows the strength of each price movement. The best trade location is when price reaches an unfair price and volume is increasing. This suggests traders may feel volume is at a higher or lower level and a breakout occurs.

On the other hand when coming into an area of unfair price, if traders are stepping back, you can see it in volume decreasing. This raises the probability of rotation back away from that unfair price and back to value where trade was facilitated.

When multiple timeframe areas of unfair price are not available, the trader/investor is relegated to look at shorter term areas of trade location. There is nothing wrong with this, but the length of the move may not be as great.

An instrument or market that moves into an area of unfair price has reached a point where it will either rotate back through the range it has just come, or it will extend vertically outside of that area of rotation and seek value at a different level. The key to rotation or vertical development lies in understanding the internals, or in volume if it happens to be a stock. A breakout of that unfair price level on increasing volume has just given you a big clue the market participants feel value is going to be found at a different level.

This is where it is important to develop along with a strategy, tactical entries. It is not the purpose of this book to proffer tactical entries, but I will offer this suggestion. When you make a tactical entry, you have made the decision the probabilities are greater for your trade to make a profit. Keeping in mind there is always a possibility you are wrong, before entering the trade, you should know where the market or instrument would have to go to prove you are wrong. That is the place where you must place a stop. After, determine if the chance of loss is within your risk parameter.

In my own trading, when I make a decision to enter a trade, it takes two clicks of the mouse. The first is the entry and just as quickly the second is the stop placement. From there the strategy and tactics apply to trade management and stop management.

I will offer one more piece of advice. If an instrument does not breakout but rotates away from an area of unfair price, it is still an opportunity to enter and ride price back to value. In this case the instrument may move slowly but it should move away from the unfair price. In the case of an instrument breaking out of an area of unfair price and seeking value at a different level away from the previous area of rotation, it is a convictive move on the part of participants. It means they have realized that value is not correct and it typically brings in a lot of volume as other participants realize the same thing. This means that a vertical development move should move quickly away from the unfair price level.

There are times when someone will try to draw in additional participants by pushing the instrument just outside of the unfair price level. If they are unable to draw in additional participants, price will rotate back through the unfair price level. This is basically a false breakout. Therefore, on any vertical development move, watch to see if volume is increasing. If so, the price should move away from your entry point in a timely fashion, allowing you to at least get a breakeven stop in, or to lock in a profit. Be wary of any instrument that breaks out and then lingers just outside of the unfair price level.

Finally, most traders and investors, having made the decision to enter this business, feel they must be in the markets all of the time. Psychologically, they feel not being in a trade is not making them money and therefore they are failing. This lack of patience leads to getting chopped up and more importantly entering trades with no idea whether it is good trade location or not. This is one of the reasons most short term traders fail. They just want to get into the heat of the trade. They want the action but none of the work. But, those are the traders who provide the liquidity and profitability for those of use who do the work, understand where trade location is and can read the internal strength or weakness of a move.

I would much rather sit for four days not trading but doing the analysis than losing capital trying to force trades, because on the fifth day my time will come. My patience will have paid off and the work I did for those four days will result in an increase in capital, not a decrease.

In summary, your methodology is how you analyze an instrument and develop a strategy. The strategy should consider all possible outcomes and what your possible actions will be. Once you see a strategy occurring, then you move in for a tactical entry.

CHAPTER 11

THE TRADE PLAN

A s PART OF THE business plan, a company will develop an Operation Plan. This plan defines how the product the company makes will be produced and monetized. For those of us in the investment arena, the Operation Plan is the Trade Plan. It is the plan we prepare each day that tells us how we will operate for that day. In order to prepare the trade plan we need to do the analysis. That analysis begins with a decision on which instruments you will trade.

To begin the trade plan, you first need to construct a foundation for the plan. The first layer of the foundation is the current positions you are holding. Your most critical decision process must be directed toward those first. This is where trade management is important. Decisions will need to be made each day on stop management, exit strategies, price development, the structure of the current trend, etc. This is important because you have capital at risk. Even if you are showing profits in your position, why allow those profits to be taken away by not managing the trade properly.

Recently, I was trading call options in Apple (AAPL). I had been in the position for a couple of days and I was showing a nice profit. However, at the close one day I noticed some weakness coming into the stock and it appeared there would be a rotation down that could be more than I would want to experience. For me, I have a real psychological issue of seeing profits evaporate because I did not manage a trade properly.

That evening, I developed my plan for the next day. It included exiting the AAPL options if the stock traded below a certain point. The next trading day the weakness I suspected showed itself and my level was broken. I exited my position and booked a very nice profit. That was the plan I came into the day with. All day AAPL traded lower. At the end of the day, I was very happy. But, the next morning AAPL opened higher and above my exit point. At that time, I didn't have a re-entry plan and experience taught me to never chase a trade. I ignored the move and went on to execute other parts of my plan for the day. Other traders might handle that trade differently. For me, I feel I can never be wrong if I make a profit on a trade. This is where the trade plan is important. It will be different for every trader.

Certainly, I could have included AAPL in my trade plan for the next day, but I didn't. Trying to chase it would have been a disaster because I would be entering a position with no plan. More importantly, by the end of that day, AAPL had traded below my exit point once again. There are thousands of opportunities in the markets each day. Investigate, analyze and then come up with a plan for each instrument that you plan to invest in for each day. You don't have to react without analysis and planning.

The second layer of the foundation will be to have instruments you expect to take positions in. These are high priority candidates that are close to fulfilling your analysis and you expect them to provide you with tactical entries in the coming day. If and when they do, you will execute tactically and they will move to the primary level for trade management.

The third layer are those instruments who you think may eventually develop into possible positions. They are basically a watch list of instruments that appear to be developing in a way that would provide an opportunity. Some of these will move to the second layer by the end of the day and some will drop off completely and be replaced by others.

I would much rather be looking at several different instruments for a good reward to risk trade than analyzing one instrument and having to deal with the psychological conflict of feeling a need to be in a trade and the resultant higher risk, lower reward trade.

My trade plan is done after the close and/or prior to the open. At times, it is even done during the market hours. I am always looking for opportunities that I can apply my strategy. Once I have sifted through some prime candidates, I set tactical alerts. When that alert goes off, I immediately move to the chart and evaluate the strength of the move and then decide if I am going to execute.

During any given day, I may have as many as twenty different instruments with alerts setup. When one goes off, I can immediately move to that instrument and investigate further to decide whether it merits looking for a tactical entry or not.

You should prepare a trade plan for each day. If you do this work, you will find the benefits far out weigh the time it takes to prepare. The plan should be short. Below are the areas that I suggest going through for each instrument or market you trade. Swing traders and longer term investors will not have to prepare a detailed plan for each day but should review the progress of trades each day and should prepare a plan for any new entries planned for the following day, along with trade management strategies.

At the top of each day plan, I put the date. Below that I have developed a form that is as follows:

MARKET CONDITIONS

It is extremely important to understand the current market conditions. After all, if the market has entered a longer term trend in one direction, that is important. Federal Reserve announcements, earnings releases, geopolitical events and economic situations should all be considered, as they can change the perception of value on market participants. Remember, in a rising or falling market, most all stocks will tend to move with the overall market. Some will react more and some less, but it is a big investment ocean. The majority of instruments will rise and fall with the tide.

Currently, I prepare a recorded Briefing for my clients at the end of each day. In that Briefing I basically give them the analysis for various Stock Indices and Metals in multiple timeframes. It is the part of the trade plan that identifies trade location, strength of the move into a support or resistance area and my probability assessment of one event occurring over another when an instrument reaches support or resistance.

In the Briefing there are many times I will suggest a market is not in an area of good trade location and to stand aside. That does not mean you ignore the market. Typically, when that occurs, I will set an alert at an area of good trade location and then move on to another instrument. When that area is reached, the alarm lets me know and then I can quickly move to it and finish the analysis as to strength or weakness of the move into the area and then look for a tactical entry.

I once had a subscriber, after listening to a Briefing, send me an email and sarcastically suggested I was telling them either the Market was going up or it was going down. I wrote him back and sarcastically said, "Yes!" What he missed was the fact I had explained the higher probability was the Market was going up, but if certain other things were to occur, it would be going down. It was a probability assessment.

WEATHER

You are probably asking yourself, why weather? The weather can affect our feelings. If it has been cloudy and rainy for a few days, it will have a dampening effect on our psychological outlook and that in turn can affect our decision process. Simply make a note as to the weather conditions for the day. You may be surprised in looking back that you can identify days that maybe you should go a little light on trading because the weather does have an impact on you.

PSYCHOLOGY

How do you feel today? If you had an argument, you may be feeling a little angry. If you don't feel well, then make a note of it.

If you feel great and are ready to strap yourself in and attack the markets, put that down. These records will give you tremendous information in going forward. If you think your psychology or how you feel does not affect trading, you are mistaken. Try this for a time, then go back and review the results. You will be surprised. Avoid trading on days when you have not performed well in the past.

CURRENT POSITIONS

Here I list each of the positions I have, where the stop is and my assessment for the coming day. I use the "if, then" statements for each positions. It basically says, if XYZ does this, then I will do that. If XYZ does that, I will do this. In this way, I don't tell the market or instrument what it is going to do. I do allow the instrument or market to tell me what it is going to do and then I have a plan for my action: exit, stay with the trade, add more, move the stop.

ANTICIPATED POSITIONS

These are instruments from the analysis that are close to possible tactical entries. In other words, entries were close to being made in the previous day but they had not quite developed tactically yet. The expectation for a tactical entry to occur in the current day is high. These may even be watchlist instruments who are close to hitting alerts I have set.

My trade plan for these are simple. I write the symbol down on the plan. From my analysis, I have a higher probability assessment of one event occurring over another. Therefore, if I think XYZ is going to continue to move higher and is close to my alert, I will write the following: If XYZ trades above X, then I will enter long with a stop at Y.

Here it is important to ask yourself one simple question and then answer it truthfully. If you expect XYZ to move higher, it is a result of analysis you have done. Where would XYZ have to go to prove your analysis wrong. That is where your initial stop will need to be placed. If that is distance is outside of your risk tolerance, then you have to make a decision as to whether to enter the trade, reduce you lot size or look for an opportunity someplace else.

You might be asking yourself, if I think XYZ is going higher, why not just enter the trade. Good question! It is because I want a stock to prove to me it is going higher before I give that stock my money. I may make slightly less on the trade but the number of profitable trades is much higher.

I know exactly where I am going to enter and where my stop will be. After the entry, if the instrument stalls, then I continue my analysis and decide on whether I want to stay with the trade or not. There have been many times, I have entered an instrument expecting it to continue trending, only to see it stall right after my entry. In these cases, I will give it some time. If it hasn't moved after a day or two, I will exit and move on to another opportunity. If trading futures, I will not give the trade days to work out. In fast moving markets, I expect the trade to move away from my entry point quickly. If it lingers and doesn't move soon after my tactical entry, then the probabilities are increasing something else may be developing.

By having all of this in front of me, I can react quickly to movements in markets and instruments. I glance at the trade plan and I know exactly what to do because of my analysis and planning.

Watchlist Instruments

These are stocks or other instruments I have been looking at for one reason or another. There a times when I will hear about a company or a market on TV that will interest me. I will analyze it and if I think it has possibilities, I will put it on the watchlist and see how it develops. Eventually, some of these will fall of, some will move up to anticipated positions and others will simply be replaced by other better opportunities.

There are some who will prefer to trade only one market or only one or two stocks. In this way, they get to know the instrument and how it trades. There is much merit in this concept. However, there are times when every instrument or stock will go into a trading range. Those ranges are difficult to trade, and usually end up causing the trader to have to stand aside for a time. It has always been my position that if my analysis works in one market, it will work in others. Therefore, rather than sit through a consolidation and do nothing, or worse force a trade, I would prefer to use my knowledge and gain additional experience by analyzing other markets or instruments.

Reward/Risk

This is a significant part of any trade plan. I keep this at the bottom of each day's plan for reference. It doesn't change with each day. It remains mostly constant. Here, you need to decide on how much you will risk on any one trade; how much you will risk on any one day; how much you will risk on any one week.

Recently, I had a stock on my watchlist that moved up to anticipated level. The next day it triggered an entry. However, it was a very high priced stock. Where my stop would have to be put was in excess of my allowance for a loss on any one trade. I felt strongly about the potential for a move and did not want to miss the opportunity, even though it was outside of my risk tolerance. I did a quick calculation and decided if I cut my normal position size down to a quarter of what it normally was, it brought the risk within my tolerance levels. I took the trade and it paid off nicely. There are times, when you will have to pass on a trade due to risk tolerance. Trust me. If you adhere to this one rule in your plan you will be happy for it. Manage risk! Manage risk! That should be your first thought before entering a trade.

You will also need to know how much you are willing to lose in any one day. There will be days when you are simply off. It seems the markets know you are coming and with every entry, they move against you. Knowing where your daily limit is and terminating your trading when that limit has been met will save you thousands of dollars in the long run. No one can be right in the markets all of the time. Knowing when it is time to take a break can prove to be a valuable part of every trade plan.

Finally, if you have accumulated losses over a couple of days and hit your weekly risk tolerance level, it is time to take the rest of the week off, step back from entries, manage the profitable trades and spend your time analyzing what is wrong with your analysis. I have done this many times. In fact, as I write this, there was a time a few weeks ago when I hit my weekly risk tolerance. It was a Tuesday and there were three trading days left in the week.

My trader mentality told me to keep trading and the week would turn around. Psychologically, I was tempted to keep going. Instead, I stepped back and stopped trading. I began to look over the positions for the last couple of days and analyzed them again and again. I wanted to find my mistake and learn from it. After a little more than a day, I found the cause. I wrote about it at the beginning of this book in the chapter on Strengths & Weaknesses. The problem was pride.

I had just come off of several weeks of stellar performance. Even the trades that did not turn out as I expected, allowed me to get out with not much loss or a slight profit. I was lured into a frame of mind that I could do no wrong. That led to anticipating what an instrument would do and taking early entries. In other words, I was telling my positions what they would do before they did them. I was violating my own analysis and tactics. The market had tempted me into believing that I could predict where an instrument would go before it came into an area of good trade location. The result was a string of losses.

It is difficult to fight your feelings. In the example above, I was doing the analysis and my feelings were telling me what was going to happen, instead of being patient and allowing the stock to prove to me what it was going to do. It resulted in early entries and the stock moving in the opposite direction.

My point here is having a plan and holding to it stopped me from continuing down a path that would have led to additional losses. Stepping back, making a note of what happened, put me back on track again.

I want to offer a word of warning here. As I stated previously, for me to enter a trade takes two clicks of the mouse. One is for entry and the second is to place a stop. Before entering a trade, I know where the market would go that would increase the probability my analysis and strategy are wrong. If the instrument reverses and begins to approach my stop, I never move it, unless the market has given me additional information that tells me my analysis is incorrect.

There is a very real temptation to out think yourself when the instrument is beginning to trade to your stop and it appears to be a weak move, suggesting it will recover. Never move your initial stop to allow the trade more room. If you are stopped out, reanalyze the instrument. Be patient. It may be you will have another opportunity to enter at lower support or the stock may trade back up and you will have another chance to enter once again. Remember, your strategy and tactics said, if it goes to this point, I am wrong. Don't second guess your analysis. On the other hand, always move your stop to breakeven to take risk off the table and then to begin locking in profits.

Periodically, I receive 911 calls from clients who moved their initial stop or canceled it completely thinking the stock would recover, only to find it just kept going. I am reminded again of my European client who allowed the instrument to continue to fall and then called to get help in recovering.

Be disciplined. Trust your work and not the market. Know the risk you are willing to take. Understand where the stock would go that would increase the probabilities you were wrong and then exit at that point. I cannot tell you how many times this strategy saved me from myself and my own psychology.

It may be difficult to take a loss but it is much better to take a small one and look to recoup it later, as opposed to taking a larger one and hoping the stock will recover.

POSITION SIZE

Position size is critical. Previously, I suggested that if you can successfully trade 10 shares of a stock, you can successfully trade 100 shares. If you can trade 100, you can trade 1000. However, assume you have evaluated a stock. You know where good trade location is, but the risk is more than you want to take. But, you feel very confident the instrument will move a good distance and you don't want to miss it. In this case, reduce the risk. You can do that by tightening your stop, or by reducing your position size. This is aptly called trade management.

Alternatively, if you find an entry and the risk is much lower than your tolerance, add to the position size to bring it to your tolerance level. It is important to remember you are in the business of making points and cents. Those points and cents accumulate and over time will provide you with a very nice living. What is most important is that you preserve your capital and not take risks that are far too great.

This is where planning is important. Set a limit on the amount you will not exceed in terms of a trade loss. When you do the analysis and a tactical entry sets up, know where it will have to go to prove you wrong. Calculate the loss. If it is within your loss tolerance and your normal position size, take the trade. If not, reduce position size or look for a trade with less risk.

There are various ways in which to manage a position. I had a surgeon who I mentored. He lived in California so he was able to get up early in the morning, put some trades on and then go to his office. He was basically a day trader trading the S&P futures.

His strategy was to enter with four futures contracts with an initial stop. If the S&P moved two points, he would exit two contracts. When it moved another two points, he would exit another contract. Finally, he let the last contract run and would place a four point moving stop. With each point the S&P rose, the stop would rise a point. In this way, he was able to make a substantial amount each day and on some days, he would come back to find the last contract had made much more than the other three. This also enabled him not to have to sit in front of the computer all day managing his trades.

I have also worked with clients who decide on a position size and then enter with the full position. As the instrument trades in the direction of their entry, they begin taking some off and booking profits. Others do the opposite. They enter small and then at certain areas will add to the position. This is my preference. That is the way I prefer to manage position size. If I add to a position, I treat it as a new entry. The same analysis, the same strategy and the same tactics apply. This allows me to take risk off the table and continue adding to my position as the trade proves profitable.

You will also have to deal with the psychology of position size. For many, it is difficult to see the dollars running up or down. This is where experience is important. If you are new to this business, begin small. Don't start in the futures markets as most do. Begin with a stock index ETF or some other instrument. Trade ten shares until you feel comfortable, then go to one hundred, then five hundred and so on. Or start with a hundred and then move up as you feel more comfortable.

It is easy to learn by using small lot sizes now. There are no commissions. Therefore, the cost of entry is where you place a stop and how much you are willing to risk on the trade.

One more comment is necessary. You don't have a profit until you exit the trade and book the profit. Even though an open position shows a profit, it is not actually a profit until you close the position. Always check and recheck your positions and stops before getting up from your desk, leaving the office or closing down for the day.

I was coaching a very competitive traveling youth soccer team. I had to leave the office for practice before the market closed. I was trading 20 NASDAQ futures contracts and I was up substantially. I decided to book the profits and exited the trade. I got ready for practice and went back to the office to see where the NASDAQ futures were trading. I was extremely surprised to see I had not exited the position. I had doubled my position. I now had 40 contracts. Needless to say, my heart was pounding. Fortunately, the NASDAQ had continued to move higher. Carefully, I took a breath and placed a sell order for 40 contracts. When they were liquidated, I looked over all of my other positions to be sure, I had placed all of my stops correctly.

While this turned out in my favor, it was a good lesson on checking positions before the close.

THE TRADE PLAN

I suggest you develop a form in your word processing program for your trade plan. You can print them off and fill them in my hand, if that is your desire. At the top should be the date. Below that will be the instruments you are trading.

1) Next describe the environment for the Market as a whole, even if you are trading individual stocks. If the Indices are rising or falling, all stocks will generally rise and fall with the Market. I always want to know in which direction the ship is headed.

2) List the current positions you have and what action you will take with each one should the instrument move in either direction. Trade the plan!

3) List the instruments you think may have the potential for tactical entries. Write down your action if and when certain levels are met. Plan the trade!

4) Finally, list instruments that are on your watchlist that have the potential to move up to the number two slot and be potential positions. Plan the trade!

5) When the opening bell rings and the action begins, all you have to do is monitor price action and internals and then act based on your plan. More importantly, Trade the plan!

6) There are many days, I have alerts set on watchlist instruments and one will go off. I simply refer to my trade plan and I know the action I will take. Trade the plan!

7) Finally, at the bottom put your profit or loss for the day on closed trades. This is the actual profit, not the paper profit. Along with the profit or loss, write a brief statement as to how you felt about the trade. Did you do something right? Put it down. Did

you miss something or do something stupid. Write it down. I promise you. If you do this work, you will begin to improve your performance dramatically.

Experience is key to becoming a great trader and investor. Ignore this part of what you do and you have thrown tremendous opportunity away to learn about yourself, your strategy and your business. Learn from your errors. Learn from your successes. Experience is the key to continued success. Do not ignore your experiences. That is your education in this business.

CHAPTER 12

THE MOST IMPORTANT CHAPTER

T HE FINANCIAL PLAN IS where Goals become reality. This is where we get specific with the numbers. Remember, the beginning of the planning process is developing a vision. What is your calling in life? Why are you entering this business? What function does your business play in reaching that vision? The Goal statement sets specific goals that you hope to achieve over a three to five year period. Those goals will lead you to fulfilling the vision you have established. The Financial Plan brings everything down to even more specific criteria. It is where we put the numbers together.

Think of the planning process as a funnel. At the top it is wide and encompasses a broad vision. As you work through the planning process it narrows more and more until you get down to actual monthly and weekly specifics. The financial plan gives us the mile markers in which to work toward the goals.

There is another purpose for the financial plan and this is the most important: control. In working with individuals, one of the questions I ask them is, "How do you know you are successful? Define success for me." The responses are always the same. They look away, pause and trying to think of what determines success. The answer is always the same. "I want to make money."

Making money does not necessarily define success. There are plenty of businesses who make money only to end up in the trash heap of failure because they didn't make enough money. Therefore, if you are investing your own money as a second business, or if you are taking the step to support yourself full time as a trader or investor, you will need to define success. Making money is not a definition of success. Making a specific amount of money is a definition of success.

Success can be defined with many different components, but the most important of those components is the financial success. After all, if we didn't have to produce income, there would be no reason to work or to risk what we have. Therefore, the development of a sound financial plan is critical to the success of your business.

The next chapter will deal with another aspect of the financial plan also and that is the control of the trader. Previously, I discussed the importance of a split personality if you are going to be trading and investing. One person needs to be the shareholder and the other the employee/trader. There are times when the shareholder will need to take control of the employee and make changes, just as the shareholder would do in any business that is not performing according to plan. The financial plan is critical to the determination of success and in alerting you when you will need to take some corrective action.

In the chapter of Strengths & Weaknesses, I discussed the importance of taking an account of all of our strengths to be able to capitalize on them and our weaknesses in order to minimize or overcome them. The financial plan will assist in showing us what we are doing right and what we are doing wrong. If you ignore this aspect, then you will be operating in the financial markets without control. Controlling the trader will raise the probability of success.

The Financial Plan can be broken down into two sections: capital plan and profit and loss. You can begin with either one. If you have a lot of capital, begin with that. If you don't have a lot of capital, begin with the profit and loss.

The person with a lot of capital available will need to decide how much of that capital they are willing to put into the business in the form of trading capital. Next, decide on what you think is an achievable rate of return. Once again, if you decide, as some I have worked with, that you can make a 300% return, you are kidding yourself and headed for disaster.

Is 300% achievable? Certainly it is and I worked with one person who has done that. However, for most of us it is not. In fact, if you can really do that, don't risk your own capital. There is a bank or hedge fund that will pay you millions a year to trade their money and make that kind of return.

It is important to remember there is a direct relationship between reward and risk. The higher your expected return, the more pressure you will be under to take higher risk positions. The most important thing you can do is to set a realistic goal. You may find later that you can do better. That is great! Once you have experience, revise your plan. If you set the goal too high, revise it downward again.

Another approach it is to decide on a number you want to make each month. Look at your capital and decide if you have enough capital to make that amount using a realistic rate of return. As an example, if you expect to make $2,000 per month and have $50,000 in capital, that is about a 50% return on capital. However, if you have $100,000 in capital, it is a 24% return. Someone with more capital can take lower risk trades but with greater position size and still make a good return on capital. Remember, the higher your rate of expected return, the greater the risk you will have to take.

Consider this. Time in the markets equals risk. The more time you spend in a position, the greater the risk. The greater the position size, the greater the risk. Markets can move overnight and surprise even the most astute trader. That is one of the most important concepts to remember. The higher the rate of return, the higher the risk you will have to take to achieve it; the more trades you will be in; and the longer your capital will be at risk.

Begin by figuring a reasonable rate of return on your capital and how much capital you will invest in your business for the first year. Then, break it down into monthly objectives and then weekly. This is extremely important. After the end of each day, track your profitability and performance against your weekly goal. This will lead you to being able to see your performance against your monthly objective and that leads to achievement of your yearly goal.

The key here is developing the plan and then tracking your performance against the plan. When you do this, you will likely see that you are performing to the objectives you established or you are not. If not, then it is time to assess what you are doing that needs to change. It is much better to find and correct your errors having lost a little capital than to ignore your performance and lose a lot of capital.

I worked with many individuals who have plenty of capital in which to work with and I worked with a few who have minimal capital. As a result, I decided to do an experiment. I opened a separate account and put $10,000 into it.

I developed a plan to manage that $10,000. I set a financial goal of 40% return at the end of twelve months. This is $4,800 profit for the year and it breaks down to $400.00 per month; $100.00 per week; and $20.00 per day. Anyone looking at this would think it simple to make an average of $20.00 per day. There were two hurdles that I encountered early in the experiment. The first was I had no leverage. Therefore, the number of stocks I had to choose from were limited to lower priced instruments. The second was the Pattern Day Trader Rule. This rule states that you must have $25,000 in an account to day trade. If you do not, you can only make three day trades in a five day period. The penalties for going over this are severe. While the Pattern Day Trader Rule does not apply to the futures markets, I wanted to stay away from them in an effort to simulate someone with lower capital and a lack of knowledge and experience. Therefore, I did not make any futures trades.

If thought that if I am teaching individuals who have limited capital, I needed to experience what they would go through.

I setup a spreadsheet with the monthly goals for each month and then cumulative objectives. After each trading day, I entered the trades. In some cases I had a day trade and marked that carefully so I could track it. After exiting a position, I booked the profit or loss on the spreadsheet. After three months, I was barely making my objectives. This really disturbed me. However, keeping with the purpose of the financial plan, I stopped trading to determine what the problem was. It didn't take long for me to see it.

Because of the Pattern Day Trader Rule, I was anticipating overnight moves. In order to avoid day trades, in some cases, I held positions looking for an additional move in the morning or anticipating a gap overnight. Often times, the market would not move overnight or would move in the opposite direction. In the past I never had to worry about day trades. If I saw a trade was not going to perform, I could exit without a thought. With this account, it was different.

As soon as I stepped back from the trading, I could see the error in my thought process. I made an immediate correction and guess what? I was able to immediately begin making profitable trades once again. Because of the day trade rule, my strategy was to hold trades overnight. That goes against my knowledge and experience. The strategy I use outlines exactly what I expect a trade to do. If it doesn't, then I get out of it. Remember, time in the market equals risk. I changed the strategy to not take trades I would normally take. I lowered the risk tolerance. In other words, I took only trades I felt had a much higher probability of success. This resulted in fewer trades and trades that were not day trades. The profits rolled in.

The key in having a financial plan was instrumental in the management, not just of the trade, but of the business. After a couple of weeks performance was not as planned. As in any business, you assess the reasons why performance is not being achieved and develop alternative strategies. That is exactly what I did. All it took was a little adaptation.

Here is the key to the success of this small account. Remember, my goal was $100.00 per week. There were a lot of times I would make $100 or more the first day of the week. If I did, the balance of the week, I sought only very low risk trades. You see, I looked at it this way. I was hired to do a job. The job was to trade $10,000 and make a 40% return or $100.00 per week. That was my goal. When I achieved it, I had done my job and the shareholder should be happy. Many times I exceeded it and the shareholder (me) was extremely happy. Once the goal was achieved, I didn't stop trading. I simply looked for greater reward to risk trades. I am very jealous, once profits have been booked, to not give them up again.

The key to success was first establishing the objective. The second was adapting my trading strategy to account for the Pattern Day Trader Rule. The third was evaluating my performance against my goal. Finally, the fourth was finding the strategy to reduce risk and increase the return.

The business process is: planning, organizing, management and control. That process is a loop. Once you reach the control function and evaluate performance, you start back an planning and go through it again, making adjustments and constantly evaluating performance.

So, if you have a small account, you can be successful. Success is more important than anything else. If you can produce a 40% return on $10,000, you can produce a 40% return on $100,000 or $1,000,000. It is just zeros. As your capital account grows, you don't have to do anything different except add zeros to the number of shares or instruments you trade.

All in all, it was a good exercise for me because it made me realize the difficulties a trader or investor may have in adjusting to the Pattern Day Trader Rule. Also, please do not think 40% is the norm. If you are beginning to manage your own money and trade, you may want to start with a lower return. Alternatively, if you have more experience, you may chose something greater than 40%. I picked that return basically at random because I felt it was realistic for me.

Imagine the trader or investor who sits down and simply begins to put trades on. There is no record keeping, no performance evaluation and no corrective actions. There is only a casual glimpse of the capital account, as it begins to dwindle and the psychological assurance that tomorrow will be better. This is the sure way to failure. Instead, develop a financial plan and force yourself to look at the truth. Either you are succeeding or you are failing. If it is success, then capitalize on what you are doing. If failure, stop and take corrective action. If the failure persists, stop again and keep doing it until success comes. Knowledge, experience and patient persistence is the key to gaining success.

I want to offer a word of caution, especially if you are just starting out with trading and investing. Whatever your capital account is, decide on a reasonable rate of return. Three hundred percent return is not reasonable. I use that number because I had a client who was convinced he could make that much money. He did not, but when he became reasonable, he was successful. You see, the important point is YOU define success or failure. Once you do that, hold yourself to it. If you set your objectives too high, then revise them. It is much better to gain success making 10% first, as opposed to losing money.

I gave a presentation on planning in a seminar. When I discussed setting up financial objectives, one person stated he didn't want to limit himself and wanted to make as much as he could. I tried to explain, whatever the objective you chose it is not a limit. It is a control function. For some reason, he couldn't see it. If you are not making an objective, then you are failing. Again, YOU set the objective. And, if you exceed the objective, give yourself a pat on the back or better, give yourself a financial reward.

If you expect to support yourself from the business, then you have to begin by figuring out how much it will take to do that. If you need $5,000 per month in income and have $5,000 in capital, that is a 1200% return on capital and for most it will be difficult to say the least. As discussed above, the trading rules are stacked against you. If you have $50,000 in capital, it is a 120% return. This is better, but then again, the amount of risk you will have to take to generate that kind of return will work against you.

Someone with a $100,000 account, coupled with knowledge and experience, will have a much better chance of making a 60% return and achieving $5,000 per month. Remember, the higher the rate or return you expect, the greater the risk you will have to take. This means more time in the market and time in the market equals risk.

Let's assume you are an individual who wants to build up a capital account. You have some capital or have been able to put together enough capital to have a $25,000 account. Your goal is to have a capital account of $125,000 at the end of five years. This then suggests you will make an average annual return of 40%. Actually, if you begin with that, you will have made much more than $125,000 at the end of five years, if you use compounding.

With $25,000 starting capital and a 40% return objective, that means you are setting an objective of making $833.00 per month or about $200.00 per week. If successful, at the end of the first month your capital account will be $25,833 or thereabouts. Recalculating return on capital, you now have a goal of $860.00 per month. The third month your capital is $26,693 and your third month objective is about $890.00.

In fact, if you compound your trading each month, at the end of the first twelve months you will have made $12,053.16, which is a 48% return on capital. If you do that year after year, your capital will grow significantly. You might be asking yourself, why rate of return matters. It matters because it will give you sense of control. It is a road map to evaluate your success or failure.

As I stated above, the relationship between rate of return and risk is extremely important. An individual who expects to make a 120% return on capital will have to take many more risks in terms of trades taken and size of trade. This will be very hard on your capital account, especially if you are beginning with a smaller amount.

Some will read these words and something inside them will whisper that they can do it. They can make 120%. They can manage risk. They will not lose. Having a positive attitude is important in any business, but realism is also important. This is a business environment where most who enter fail. The number is around 92%. It is the only business that you enter and other people are trying to take your money. That is the only way they succeed. Competition is fierce. I cannot stress the importance of setting specific financial goals that are realistic.

Do not skip the preparation of the financial plan. If you do anything, draft it and put it in writing. It is the means in which you will control yourself and your business. It will help to bring success.

THE FINANCIAL PLAN PROCESS

First you will need to set your financial goals. Remember to keep time as a key criterion. Most businesses will look out five years and decide where they want to be at the end of five years. They plan backwards to the present year. The current year then becomes their action plan to achieve the goal at the end of the year. If it is achieved, then they move to the second year plan.

Remember the planning process is a fluid process. You will change your plan each year on a major basis, but realistically you should be reviewing it on a daily basis and making adjustments, as you deem necessary. Once you have created the plan, it is not cast in stone. It should adapt with you and with the markets.

Because the business of trading and investing can be volatile, lets start with a three year plan. Go back to the goals you established. Beginning with the third year out, quantify those goals in terms of money. How much will you have to make in the third year to achieve your goal? Remember to put in expenses. You will have expenses such as a charting program, data feed charges, etc.

Now do the same thing with the second year. Keep in mind that it must be relational to the third year. There must be a realistic jump between years two and three.

Once that is complete, prepare the same assumptions for year one. If you have done it correctly, you should have a reasonable progression from year one through year three. With each step, question yourself. Are these numbers reasonable? If not, then you will have to adjust the numbers or adjust the goals you set for yourself. I cannot stress how important this aspect of the planning process is. I will discuss it more in the next chapter titled Controlling the Trader, but this is the main mechanism in which you will be able to define success or failure. More importantly, it is the mechanism that will tell the shareholder the trader needs a good talking to and a change in behavior.

Now that you have the financial objectives set for the three years, take the first year and break that down into months. Those will be your monthly goals. I also suggest you break those down into weekly goals. I have known some who take the next step and look at what they need to achieve each day, but that can lead to putting yourself under too much pressure. Because we have to assume there will be losses, you can have a day or two of losses and make your weekly goal back in one day with one trade. Alternatively, you can work all week and achieve your weekly goal and just before the market closes on Friday, you can lose it all. Important here is the concept of protecting your profits. Additionally, you don't want to be under pressure to trade every day. That will open the problem of taking higher risk trades. Rather, be patient and look for the high reward, low risk trades.

Out of all of the clients I have worked with in the past, those who went on to achieve success paid much attention to their financial plan and held themselves accountable to it.

CAPITAL

Your capital is where the rubber meets the road. You can go through the entire process above and then look at your capital and decide you simply don't have enough to achieve those goals. Your rate of return is simply not realistic. There are two things you can do from here. Revise your goals so they are realistic, or increase your capital. For most, increasing capital is easier said than done.

One way to increase your capital is to simply take it out of some other savings vehicle. For some that may be easy but for others, more difficult. If you have it, great. If you don't, then it is another matter.

Another possibility is to borrow the funds. However, that can be digging a hole for yourself that will be difficult to get out of. First, what is the interest rate you will have to pay? If it is a high rate of interest, which is what any bank will charge in the current lending environment, then your hurdle to make the interest rate and a profit will be too steep. The worst thing would be to borrow at say 10% and try to make 20%. That would give you a 10% profit on the bank's money. However, if you don't make over 10%, then you are compounding your losses. Further, if you lose money, then you are really in trouble.

I have seen two other possibilities used by clients. One is to go to family and friends. If they have excess cash, it is most likely in a savings account accumulating a whopping 1% return per year. Think about offering 5%. By doing this, your hurdle rate is only 5%. Therefore, if you make 10%, you have made 5% above your cost of capital. Also, the family and friends who funded your business are getting 4% more than the bank is paying them.

Certainly, there is more risk for the individuals lending you the money, but if you have a good track record, then the risk is minimal. If you have no previous performance, then I suggest you not borrow and try to figure a way to build a track record and gain the knowledge and experience necessary.

If you have sufficient capital, then decide on a realistic rate of return you want to make. Bring that down to yearly, monthly, weekly and daily objectives. If you exceed that return, revise it. If you are not achieving it, revise it or figure out what you are doing that needs to change.

On the other hand, if you are a beginner and have had some initial success, decide on where you want to be at the end of three years in terms of capital and rate of return. Beginning with a $25,000 and expecting to make $75,000 is not realistic. As I have said previously, there is a direct relationship between reward and risk.

If you have a record of making 30% per year on a $10,000 account and want to make $75,000 per year, then you need more capital. There are various ways to get that capital. A track record of 30% ROC would need $250,000 in capital to produce $75,000.

Trading is a business of risk management. We have to take on risk to make money, but it is our duty to preserve that capital. If we don't, we are out of business.

Whatever the size of your account and whatever your level of experience is, don't bet the farm on any trade or any strategy. Take your time and manage risk. If you are just coming to this business, remember my theory of zeros. Begin small. Produce the return on capital. As your capital increases, add a zero to your position size.

Your job is to make a certain amount of money each day, week and month. That is all. Some months will be banner and you will far exceed your objective. Others will not be so great. The important point is overall are you achieving success?

Two years ago I started a new Fund with a partner. Our strategy was to develop various option strategies. Because the Markets can change behavior, we developed and are still developing strategies that can perform better in various market environments. As a result, our initial strategy was to limit risk as we tested those strategies. Some lost a little and some made a little. The losers were tossed aside and the winners were capitalized. For two years, returns were limited. However, because we managed risk first, the returns are beginning to come through. Now, we can set objectives for profitability and expansion.

Just as we did with this Fund, you should do with your capital. Decide on a strategy. Limit risk. Test your strategies. Develop successful tactics. Limit risk. Dump non-performing trades and let the winners run. To do that you need an objective that is achievable each day you go to work.

If you can consistently produce a reasonable return, capital will be available to you, if you want it.

Summary

One of the most important steps you will take in developing a business plan for your trading and investing is the financial plan. As you will see in the next chapter, this is the means in which you will be defining success or failure. It is the system in which warning flags will come up, sirens will go off and a time when the shareholder you will have to take the trader you to the woodshed.

- Begin with setting specific financial goals. Below are some statements for consideration in developing those objectives.

- Decide on how much capital you have or are willing to commit to your trading and investing business.

- Decide on a reasonable rate of return that you expect to achieve. This will depend on your knowledge and level of experience. If you have little experience, you should begin with a very low return on capital. Remember, you are going to be entering a business where you will have to educate yourself and gain experience at your cost. Keep the cost of that education low.

- Multiply the rate of return by your capital account and that is the amount of money you will set as an objective to make in the first twelve months.

- Divide the amount by twelve to get your monthly goals and then by four to get your weekly goals.

- Decide on position sizing. This will vary based on the size of your capital account and your level of experience. You can always increase your position size based on your success.

- Assuming your first year is successful, decide on a reasonable rate of return for your second year. Also, decide on the capital you will have. If you think you will want more capital, then decide on how you will acquire that capital. If your capital is sufficient, then calculate the amount of money will make at the end of the second year.

- Do the same thing for the third year, as you did above. Then, compare your performance at the end of three years to where you expected to be according to your goals statements and your vision. If you need to revise any section of the plan, do so.

Based on the above goals and objectives, we now have the basis to plan our capital properly.

The most important part of the planning process is what you do going forward. The environment for all businesses change. Performance for all businesses change. Therefore, you must change and adapt your plan as necessary. I gave an example previously of what happened to me when I did an experiment with a $10,000 account. I prepared a detailed plan for that account. The first two months fell short of my objectives. I immediately stopped and re-evaluated. I was sure I had overcome the problems. I began again and success was found once more.

CHAPTER 13

CONTROLLING THE TRADER

THE MAIN PURPOSE OF planning for any business is to achieve a vision of what we want to accomplish. To reach that vision we establish goals and objectives. It is the success of achieving those goals and objectives that bring forth the fruit of the vision. Therefore, it is most important that our goals and objectives be specific and achievable. Along with this, it is even more important to establish control procedures. Control procedures tell us if we are on track to achieve the success we have defined.

Now that you have completed the financial plan, it is time to put in some control procedures. You cannot develop control procedures, unless you have completed the previous steps in the planning process. After all, control means monitoring and evaluating performance against the standard that has been set. In the previous chapter we established those performance mechanisms. They are the financial goals and objectives. By monitoring the progressive success of our performance, we know whether we are on track to achieving success or not. If not, then it is most important to take corrective action. Corrective action is important to any business but even more important in the business of trading and investing. Because you are not achieving your objectives does not mean you are failing. It means you need to take corrective action. Not taking corrective action means you are on the path to failure.

Imagine starting a business. You go through all of the planning, get it setup, and start operating. You developed a budget that determines whether you will be financially successful or not. Now, consider the business owner who ignores that plan, does not keep track of his profitability and performance. How will he know if he is successful or not. The financial plan told him what success would be and what was failure. In most cases, that business owner would be doomed to failure.

The business owner who plans properly and then evaluates actual performance against his plan knows exactly where he stands and then takes immediate corrective action if he is not performing. That business owner has a much higher degree probability for success than the former. It is the same for the business of trading and investing.

So, why is it that most traders tune out when it comes to planning properly? Why is it that some traders plan, but then put the plan in a drawer and never look at it again? I can only surmise those individuals are looking to make quick, easy money and do not want to do the work to be successful.

Perhaps psychologically, they don't want to face the fact that they are not achieving success. After all, who wants to look in the mirror each day and know they lost money. It is much easier to shrug it off and tell ourselves we will be back tomorrow and it will be better. The ease of entry in this business brings out complacency on the part of the trader/investor. He/she doesn't feel they have to plan properly and control their business.

If the first reason for not facing our performance is psychological, then the second reason I attribute to simple laziness. They do not want to do the work. This is the main cause of failure that I have found, not just in people I have worked with, but in myself as well. It is much easier to get up after the markets close and go do something else. If there is a loss for the day, who wants to look at it? No one. It is much easier to soothe our feelings and emotions in some other way and convince ourselves we will do better tomorrow. Facing the losses. Facing the mistakes. Analyzing what we did wrong is the hard part. Figuring out how to improve performance is difficult and takes time and effort.

Tomorrow comes and then another tomorrow and another. Finally, there is not much left in the investment account and a major decision needs to be made. Do you close the business or continue to invest more in a losing operation? I have seen many people leave this business because they didn't hold themselves accountable. They did not stop trading and try to evaluate what they were doing wrong. They blew up their account.

PERFORMANCE REVIEW

The performance review is one of the most critical function you can do to be successful in this business. We must learn to take our losses and mistakes seriously. It was not bad luck. It was bad planning. It was poor execution. It was poor stop management. It was greed. It was psychological factors. Whatever the reason, you as a trader must understand the importance of the performance review.

If you were to give your money to someone else to trade for you, would you want that person to have certain goals and objectives? Would you want that person to have specific controls on your money so it was not lost completely? Would you want that person to stop trading your money if he lost a certain amount? I am sure the answer to the questions is quite strongly a yes. If that is the case, then why do most traders, who trade their own money not do the things they would expect someone else to do? Why is it we let ourselves off easy? How come traders and investors lose money only to get up, brush themselves off and think they can come back the next day without even reviewing their performance?

The performance review does not need to be lengthy. In fact it can be short and to the point. Simply put a performance review can be the following:

- How did I trade today?
- How much money did I win or lose today?
- What mistakes did I make today?
- What things did I do well today?
- What did I learn today?
- What was my psychological frame of mind today?
- How did I perform according to my plan?
- What corrective action do I need to take?

The answer to those questions can give you incredible advantages in your trading. Think about what the results will be. You will constantly be learning, refining, controlling and disciplining yourself for better trading. You will become a professional.

Success or Failure

Speaking of a performance review, have you thought about what is the definition of success or failure in the business of trading or investing? How do you define success or failure? Is success defined in more winning trades than losing trades? I know traders who have many more winning trades than losing trades, but they do not make money. Psychologically, they cannot stand to see the potential for profits be eroded by a retracement or rotation so they pull the plug on winning trades early, but then again those same traders will sit on losing trades hoping and praying the market comes back to take them out at breakeven.

Taking it a step farther, if you are going to have a performance review, that assumes you have something to review your performance against. There must be a standard, or better yet, a structure for your business that you operate within. Most people who enter the business of trading or investing do it after they have become extremely successful in another business. Yet, they enter trading with no formal business plan, no understanding of how to determine success or failure. Without success criteria, how would you know when to take corrective action.

Corrective action, now that is a thought! I wonder how many traders even think about it, or do they just brush off losses thinking tomorrow will be another day? The trader who takes the business seriously, who plans properly, who sets goals and objectives, and evaluates his performance and then takes corrective action is a professional trader. That is the trader who will succeed in a highly competitive business. That is the trader who will persevere through difficult times, only to emerge stronger, smarter, and more successful.

If you do not have success criteria established, and if you do not have a performance review with the goal of learning from your mistakes and capitalizing on your success, then you are not a professional trader and you will not succeed. You will become one of the statistics of those 92% who fail. You could not succeed in any business without proper planning and control. The most profitable times in my trading are when I stop because I am not meeting my objectives. The resulting evaluation and strategic changes result in larger profits.

It takes work to be successful. Clicking the mouse and getting in a trade is fun. There is a competition. There is a psychological rush when the trade moves in your direction, and when you do book some profits, you feel exhilarated. But, eventually the losses come, and then the bad feelings. How you deal with those feelings and how you react to your winning and losing can set you apart and make you an overall success as a trader.

The work is not done during the trading day. The work is done at night in review. You need to look at all aspects of the trading day. This includes the action of the market. Look at how it developed in terms of the longer timeframe. Look and interpret the market internals. Try to determine what signal they are sending on where the market may go in the upcoming day. Set a strategy for the new day based on your work When you come into the new day, you know exactly what to expect and only have to execute properly. If the market throws a curve, which it sometimes does, and you cannot adopt a good strategy, then step aside until a good strategy can be implemented.

In addition to the market analysis, you must measure your performance. Make notes on how your trade during the day compared to your trade plan. Note if you did not execute properly. Make notes if you did not strategically analyze the market properly. Do the work it takes to understand where your mistakes were and more importantly what successes you had. Remember you want to minimize your mistakes and maximize your successes. Take a psychological assessment also. Many times you will find, while the strategy was correct and the tactics were good, your psychology was such that you were not in a position to trade effectively.

Finally, look at your overall performance in relation to your financial objectives. If you are meeting or exceeding those goals, then capitalize on what you have done in the past. Don't take on more risk. Protect those profits.

In summary, if you want to be a professional and you want to be successful, you must do a performance review each day.

TRADE JOURNAL

The trade journal is the recording mechanism for the performance review. I have separated it into its own section because it is very important. Thinking about your mistakes, successes, psychological outlook, planning for the next day and recording your profits and losses is one thing. Actually putting them on paper is another.

The trade journal can be any form that you create yourself. It should include the following:

YOUR STRATEGY FOR THE DAY

You should write a brief analysis as to your strategy coming into the day. It should include a statement as to the Development of the market, and where the market is in relation to that Development. You should outline a primary strategy and a secondary strategy. At times, you may even adopt a strategy of standing aside. There is nothing wrong with this, and it may be very smart at times. This can be done in just a few sentences. If your strategy is to stand aside, you might say something like, "The market is trading in the middle of a range and is very choppy. This is not an area of good trade location. Therefore, I will stand aside until the market reaches one of the extremes of the larger timeframe I have been monitoring". Your strategy sets the tone for the day. It may change as the day progresses, but you are coming into the trading day prepared.

Another statement to make in the strategy is, if the market does this, I will do that. If the market does that, I will do this. If the market does neither, I will stand aside and re-analyze. At the end of the day review your strategy against how the market performed.

Charts of your trades

You should mark a chart with every trade you make. It should show the entry point, your initial stop placement, and how you managed the trade and the stops.

Trade description

Write a sentence or two on why you took the tactical entries you did and especially what your psychological outlook was at the time you took the trade. Your psychology will have a lot to do with your performance. If your are not mentally ready for the day, take the day off.

Exit strategy

Show where you exited the trade and why.

Profit and Loss

Keep a spreadsheet of your profit and loss for each day. You should be able to total it by the day, week and month so you can see your progress in meeting your financial objectives.

Performance

Calculate your performance for the day against your financial plan. Did you meet your daily goal? If not, why? Learn from the losses. If you made or exceeded your goal, analyze why? Learn to capitalize on your successes and try to repeat them. The worst thing you can do is get up from a day of investing and ignore your actions during that day and the results of those actions.

At times it will even be beneficial to make notes of different ideas you have, or if you did not trade, exactly what you saw. It is this information that you keep that will help you to avoid the things that caused you to lose money and capitalize on the things that brought you success. The journal will also help you refine your trade plan and look for new and exciting tactics.

The most important aspect is it will help you keep control of the financial end of your business. If you are not making money, you will know it and because you have to put your losses in the journal, you cannot ignore them.

The Woodshed

Einstein said the definition of insanity is doing the same thing over and over and expecting a different result. Many times I have seen traders do exactly the same thing over and over. Each day they come back with a new energy and endeavor to change the results. They talk themselves into believing one more day and everything will turn out differently. Unfortunately, the results are the same.

Everyone goes through a time period when nothing seems to go the right way. Psychologically, we tell ourselves it will be better tomorrow. It will always be better tomorrow. The key to success in any business is to recognize if the business is not performing to plan, then it is time to step back and figure out what needs to be changed. In the business of trading and investing, stepping back means to stop trading.

I was talking to a trader. He explained that he was having difficulty with his trades. He said had set his risk tolerance on each trade but was getting stopped out and then the stock would move in the direction of his trade. I asked him what lot size he was trading. Obviously, it was too large. I suggested he reduce his lot size and extend his stop to allow for a rotation. I think the psychological lure of making larger returns outweighed his ability to manage risk. He later had to leave the business. I felt bad because I really thought he had the making of a professional trader. I feel sure one day he will be back. It was a learning experience for him.

If you persist, and the losses continue to mount, it is time for the shareholder to take the trader out to the woodshed and have a good discussion.

In my personal experience, when I go through a time period of losses and cannot seem to turn the corner, it doesn't take much for me to stop trading. After all, why would you want to continue to see your capital account drained? Looking back, the most profitable times in my trading and investing career have come just after I stopped trading. There are lots of reasons for the losses, or lack of performance according to the plan.

THE PLAN IS TOO OPTIMISTIC

In this case, you are probably profitable but simply not reaching your financial goals. Revise the plan. Remember, your job is to come back tomorrow. If you don't manage risk because you are trying to make too much, you will lose your capital.

YOUR METHODOLOGY IS FAILING

This has happened several times to me. Markets are living organisms. They are made up of humans who trade and invest based on their feelings and emotions and those feelings and emotions change. In this case, analyzing your methodology and refining it will likely help you turn the corner. Take the time to step back and revise how you analyze the markets and develop a strategy.

YOU ARE LAZY

Yes, that is correct. If you come into the day without a sound strategy, then you have set yourself up for failure. If you don't do the analysis work first, then you will not be prepared for what the market will do. If you get up from your desk after the markets close, and do not study your trade(s) and the market, then you have set yourself to fail. This is one of the greatest problems with most traders. They fail to analyze the markets and plan for the coming day. Remember, most of your work will come in the analysis. If the market then moves according to the strategy you developed, then you can find a tactical entry. That entry takes only the time necessary to click a mouse. What will you do with the rest of your time?

Your tactical entries are bad

Implementation of a strategy is critical. Executing tactically is just as critical. What would signal for you to enter a market or an instrument? Once you enter, where would that instrument go to prove your analysis wrong? Did you put a stop in that place, or did you move your stop thinking the instrument would reverse? Do you fall into the trap of having a feeling the market is getting ready to move in a specific direction and then enter expecting the move? This is a mistake many traders make and I have made myself.

You felt bad

This can involve physical sickness or feeling bad psychologically. In both cases, you shouldn't be trading. Psychologically feeling bad for whatever reason can be detrimental to the health of your capital. Therefore, if you really don't feel like working for the day, don't. At the most, go into the office and do some work but stay away from the trading platform. Come back another day when you feel better.

The environment changed

This is important. We do not trade in a box. We trade in a world in which economic and geopolitical events will have a tremendous effect on the perception of value by participants in various markets and instruments. Recognize when the environment is changing and then step back and adapt.

FEELING YOU HAVE TO TRADE

This is more psychological than anything else. If you have made the decision to enter the business of trading and investing, then you are relying on a certain amount of income. It is natural to look at various instruments and try to get in on a trade to make some money. This causes forced trades in areas of bad trade location, or poor analysis. When you feel you have to make money and must be in a trade, that is the time to get up and walk away.

Whatever the reason, there will come a time when you simply need to stop what you are doing because it is not working. The most profitable action you can take is to step back, analyze your own performance, figure out what the problem is and then correct it.

Periodically, I have to stop and reassess. Most of the time it is because the environment of the markets has changed. Even if trading a stock and the environment changes, the stock will be affected. In a bear market, most all stocks decline. In a bull market, even the poor performers move higher in anticipation of improved economic conditions.

SUMMARY

If you have followed through with this chapter and established financial objectives, then you now have a means in which to evaluate performance. The critical aspect will be to monitor that performance and if successful, continue doing what is giving you that success. If you are not being successful, then stop what you are doing, evaluate everything, set a new course and then begin again. If you are not successful, STOP! Analyze and evaluate performance.

Set parameters for yourself. Anyone who manages a business sets a plan and then follows the plan. Chart your course to the results you expect and then follow it. If you get off course, do what is necessary to get back on course. Never, never, never shrug off losses. Pay attention to them. They are the cost of you developing knowledge of the markets and experience navigating them. Losses are valuable lessons.

As we were developing new option strategies for the Fund we had put together, we never invested more than 10% of the capital at any one time. In most cases, there were only one option per trade. It is only after success that more capital will be committed and larger position sizes. That is risk management.

The Control Plan should state exactly what you will do to control yourself if you exceed a loss in any one trade.

- What will you do if you exceed your loss for any one day?
- What will you do if you exceed a loss on an average of five days?
- What records will you keep?
- What type of trade journal will you keep?
- When will you stop trading completely and seek help, or revise what you are doing?
- When will you revise your business plan due to unexpected success or unexpected failure?

CHAPTER 14

IMPLEMENTATION PLAN

WHEN I STARTED THIS book, I explained my vision was to have a successful business that allowed me to spend more time with my family and work from my home. I can tell you through investing and trading, I have achieved that vision. It was not always easy, and at times it is still not, but I persisted. With each failure and each loss, I was intent on learning from it and not making the same mistakes over and over.

The planning process for a trader and investor begins with realizing your vision. What is it that you want? Why are you going into this business? Where do you see yourself in three years? Next, you have to evaluate your strengths and weaknesses and take assessment of them. A study of the trade and investment environment should be completed, and then an organizational plan put together.

The operating plan for an investor is basically the methodology that will be used to analyze the markets and develop a trade strategy. This is normally the trade plan. It is critical to success is the development of a strategy and tactics.

Finally, a financial plan is developed. This begins with looking out twelve months and preparing a twelve month budget. Next, a second and third year budget is produced. This will establish where you will be at the end of the three year period. You also now have the means in which to control the business and trader from a financial perspective.

Finally, there is the implementation plan. This is the short term action plan that will get the business moving forward. It is an action list of items that need to be accomplished before the business begins operation. In fact, the implementation plan may be carried forward into the operation of the business.

As part of my implementation plan, I have five pages of a journal that I list out on each page the day and date. Each day I add a new day and date so there is always a running five day action plan. In this way, things I need to do a couple of days from now can go on the day I need to do them or remember them. This includes key announcements that may impact the determination of value on the part of market participants. If I am invested or considering investing in a stock and an earnings announcement is on the horizon, I want to remember when it will occur.

When you first start the implementation plan, you should list all of the action items that will need to be completed. In fact, you can probably begin that list at the beginning of the planning process. Of course, everyone's implementation plan will be different, depending on where you are in establishing your business.

Some examples of what can be in the action plan are as follows:
- Decide on office space.
- Acquire necessary furniture to put in the office.

- Decide on computer equipment.
- Acquire backup internet access.
- Decide on battery backups in case the electricity goes out.
- Decide on charting program.
- Open account at brokerage firm.
- Fund brokerage account.
- Develop a methodology for a sound strategic approach.
- Develop and test tactical entries.
- Decide on markets to be traded or instruments to be traded.
- Decide on how many contracts (shares) to be traded and when to increase or decrease.
- If trading stocks, decide on how to screen various shares.

The implementation plan for each individual will differ. Some will already have an office setup and others may need to establish one. Most will work out of their homes. Where you locate your office is important. First, you will be spending many hours there, analyzing markets and instruments, studying and increasing your knowledge of analytical techniques, and in watching the markets and instrument develop as each day progresses.

If you still have another job, then your work will begin when you return home or early in the morning before going to work. Having a space where you will not be interrupted will be important because the decisions you make will have an impact throughout the day. More importantly, you will not be home to make changes if necessary.

If you are already trading and have implemented most of the above, then spend time developing a financial plan. More importantly, hold yourself accountable to that plan. It will help you manage risk and improve performance.

I have been trading for over 30 years. Periodically, I get into a losing streak. Have the determination to stop and figure out what corrective action to take. Reduce your position size until the winners start increasing. Keep educating yourself and look for new tactics and strategies. We work in a changing environment. Therefore, we must be ready to change and adapt with that environment.

AUTHOR BIOGRAPHY

Joe Mertes received an undergraduate BS degree in Political Science from Belmont Abbey College and a Master of Business Administration Degree from Wake Forest University. He began his career in private equity, building a venture capital firm that specialized in the analysis, structure and acquisition of various business entities. Capital formation, strategic business planning and control functions were key areas of responsibility. From venture capital Joe moved into working with troubled businesses through the restructure of balance sheets and capital formation. In each of these ventures he derived strategic plans based on an understanding of the development of various markets.

In 1987 Joe concentrated on investing, trading techniques and money management. Over the last twenty years he has managed significant accounts for investors and c onsulted with individuals and businesses. Currently he is responsible for the training and education of individual investors globally. Joe has assisted traders, investors and institutions on the importance of establishing a business approach to the trading arena. He is currently a partner in a small hedge fund, consultant, educator and author. Having been published in Stocks & Commodities Magazine, he now offers to clients his analysis through The Markets in Development Briefing.